DOLLS
KIDS CAN
MAKE

SHEILA McGRAW

FIREFLY BOOKS

To Pamela Anthony

Edited by Sarah Swartz
Big photos by Joy von Tiedemann
Design, how-to photos and cartoons by Sheila McGraw
Typesetting by Parker Typesetting, London Ontario

Canadian Cataloguing in Publication Data

McGraw, Sheila
   Dolls kids can make

ISBN 1-895565-75-8 (bound) ISBN 1-895565-74-X (pbk.)

1. Dollmaking – Juvenile literature.
2. Handicraft – Juvenile literature. I. Title.

TT175.M34 1995   j745.592'21   C95-931474-1

A FIREFLY BOOK

Published by:

Firefly Books Ltd.
250 Sparks Avenue
Willowdale, Ontario, Canada
M2H 2S4

Published in the U.S. by:

Firefly Books (U.S.) Inc.
P.O. Box 1325
Ellicott Station
Buffalo N.Y.
14205

Printed and bound in Canada

Contents

Getting Started

Little girls love them. Adults collect them. Even boys are learning to enjoy them. They can be your loyal companion, your good friend and your best listener. Everyone should have one. They've been around since the beginning of civilization, but never have dolls been more popular than right now!

This book will show you how to make eleven great dolls. Some are perfect for hugging and cuddling. Others are ornaments to be admired, to decorate a room, or to brighten a Christmas tree. This book includes both traditional and modern dolls, made with exciting, up-to-date materials and methods.

Organizing

Take some time to look through this book and decide which doll you'd like to make first. When you have decided, read over the instructions once to find out if the project is the right skill level for you. At the front of the book, the projects are easy. As you go through the book, they become more advanced. Reading the instructions first will also help when you are making your doll, because you'll know what's coming.

Next, collect all of the materials that you will need. This will save you frustration when you are in the middle of the project. When you work on the project, be sure not to skip any steps except the steps marked "*Optional*", if you choose not to include them.

Tools

Most of the dolls need only a small amount of sewing which can be done by hand. However, two projects, Cool Dudes and the Double Doll (Little Red Riding Hood and the Big Bad Wolf), require a lot of sewing and will take a long time to sew by hand. These require a sewing machine. If you have never sewn with a machine before, these projects are a great way to learn. Be sure that there is an adult available to help.

The dolls that require machine sewing have several pattern pieces that need to be photocopied or traced onto paper and cut out. These projects have diagrams to guide you in pinning and cutting the patterns and fabrics.

Use sharp scissors for cutting fabric, but watch your fingers!

Craft glue is recommended for sticking parts together. If you have experience with a glue gun and can find someone to supervise you, a glue gun is faster than craft glue and just as good. Beware! Glue guns are hot and can cause serious burns when not used properly.

Look it up

If you come across any materials, sewing or cutting terms that you don't understand, see the Glossary at the back of the book.

Hair

SYNTHETIC

Buy this hair at a craft store. Its shiny, curly texture looks real and works well on ornamental or realistic dolls. It can be glued or sewn in place and usually comes with its own instructions. See the potpourri dolls on page 32, steps 1 through 3, for an easy way of attaching the hair to a styrofoam ball head.

YARN

Using yarn or rope is probably the most popular method of making hair for hand crafted dolls. It is a very good method, with the wide selection of colors and textures of yarn now available. For examples, see Terry Baby on page 8, the Wacky Witch and Paper Angel on pages 18 and 19.

FAKE FUR

Fake fur comes in many different colors, textures and lengths and it can add comical and cute fluffy hair while it covers up a knot or sewing on the doll's head. Cut a circle of the fur and sew or glue it in place. For examples, see Little Guy on page 8, Baby, Baby, Oh Baby on page 42 and Cool Dudes on page 48.

Eyes

SAFETY

Why do small children love to chew on the eyes of dolls? Maybe it's the taste. Maybe the little kid is teething. Always make sure the eyes on your doll are safe and securely attached, if it is for a young child or infant.

FRENCH KNOTS

French knots make small dots for eyes that are not only cute but safe for babies.

Pick up a tiny stitch next to the thread. Wind thread around point of needle three times.

Hold wound thread together and pull needle until tight. Draw needle through fabric close to the knot. Tie off.

BUTTONS

Buttons have always been used as eyes. They give a doll an old-fashioned, handmade look. Mismatched buttons and thread can add charm to a doll's face. Buttons are not safe on a doll that is for a baby.

Heads

WOVEN COTTON

Suitable for cloth dolls, rag dolls and mop dolls, these doll heads with their cotton faces and yarn hair look both natural and traditional. For instructions on making your own woven-cotton head, see Terry Baby steps 10 through 14, beginning on page 13.

PANTI-HOSE

Using panti-hose to make a doll's head means very little cutting and sewing because the panti-hose stretches to become the size and shape you want. Panti-hose material is also very strong, but to prevent snags, file your nails! For examples, see the Wacky Witch on page 18, the Granny dolls on page 36 and Baby, Baby, Oh Baby on page 42.

STYROFOAM

Styrofoam balls can be purchased in many different sizes at craft stores. Use a size that fits and suits your doll. The styrofoam ball can be covered with a piece of panti-hose to give it a flesh tone. For examples, see the Paper Angel on page 19 and the lacy, potpourri dolls on page 30.

CRAFT EYES

Craft eyes are safe for small children if they are properly attached to heavy fabric. These eyes are available at craft stores.

Craft eyes are plastic with a post on the back. Cut a very small hole on the right side of the doll's face. Push the post through.

On the wrong side, push the grommet all the way onto the post.

PAINTED EYES

Use T-shirt paint to make colorful, chunky dots for eyes. T-shirt paint eyes are safe for babies. See Little Guy on page 8.

If you want a more realistic paint job, choose acrylic or fabric paints and a small fine brush for more detail. You can even paint the full face if you like. See Red Riding Hood on page 58.

GOOGLY EYES

Googly eyes are clear plastic with a moveable black disc inside. These eyes are either glued in place or sewn on like buttons. They are sold in most craft and sewing supply stores and they come in a variety of sizes. Googly eyes are not safe for babies.

Three Little Softies

A Collection of Small Dolls

Huggable, squeezable, soft and washable, these three little dolls have a lot in common. They are all cleverly made from easy-to-find items that you probably already have in your house – a cotton sock, a pair of stretchy gloves and a terry facecloth. They're so cute and impressive that no one will guess what they're made from, or that you whipped them up in just an hour or two!

These soft cottony babies are the perfect gift for a baby shower or an infant. Moms appreciate them as take-along toys for toddlers and your friends will love them as locker mascots and computer companions. They're great for bazaars too. Inexpensive, simple and loveable, they'll get snapped up right away!

Top left: Terry Baby, page 12. Bottom left: Little Guy, page 10. Below: Snow Baby, page 15. Doggie not included.

How to do it

Little Guy

Little Guy is made from those small, very stretchy, one-size-fits-all gloves. He is very fast to make, because the glove is folded in a clever way. Make this doll in bright colors, white or black. Whichever color you choose, he's a cute little fluffy headed guy.

Finished Size

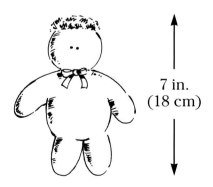

7 in. (18 cm)

Time: One hour

Words that you don't understand? See the Glossary at the back of the book.

What You Need

Materials
• pair of small, stretchy, one-size-fits-all gloves
• 3 handfuls of stuffing
• matching thread
• small scrap of fake fur
• 2 eyes (see pages 6 and 7)

Tools
• scissors
• sewing needle
• ruler
• compass

Optional
• wooden spoon
• craft glue
• ½ yd. (.5 m) narrow satin ribbon

1 Turn back the cuff on one glove until you can see the edge that is sewn down. Carefully cut into *one* layer of the cuff just above the sewing line. Continue cutting close to the sewing until the cuff is free.
Repeat with the second glove.

2 LEGS: On one glove, push the two outside fingers (not the thumb) into the fingers beside them (the two middle fingers).
Repeat with the other glove.

3 On one glove, on the opposite side to the thumb just below the wrist-ribbing, cut an up-and-down slit ½ in. (1 cm) long.
Repeat with the other glove.

4 ARMS: Put one of the gloves on your hand, putting two of your fingers into each glove finger and the thumb in its usual spot.

Now put your gloved hand into the other glove, slipping the thumb through the hole in the side and the fingers into the two legs. (You will probably need to feel around to find the openings.) The thumbs are the arms.

5 Stuff the arms, pushing stuffing through the hole in the inside glove. Add stuffing to the legs if desired. Then stuff the body. The handle of a wooden spoon is great for pushing stuffing into hard-to-get-at places.

Optional: Stitch the openings at the tops of the legs closed. Turn under and sew the cut edge around the arm.

7 Stuff the head tightly. Close the top of the head by sewing a running stitch near the edge of the ribbing and gathering it tightly. Tie off.

6 HEAD: Hand sew a running stitch around the bottom of the ribbing. Pull it tight, gathering the neck. Tie off securely.

8 For the hair, cut a 2½ in. (6.5 cm) circle of fake fur, or use a pom-pom. Sew or glue it to the top-center of the head.

Sew, paint or glue the eyes to the face. (Read about eyes on pages 6 and 7.) Tie a satin ribbon around the neck, if you wish.

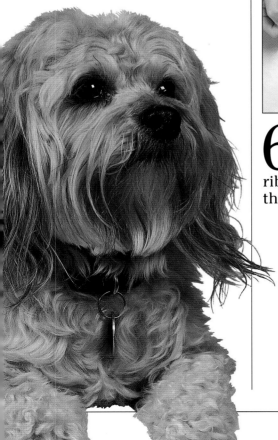

Terry Baby

The nappy terry finish of a facecloth combined with a woven cotton head and wooly hair make this doll extra cuddly. Terry Baby's head is easiest if it is sewn on a sewing machine, while the body is sewn by hand. These heads can also be purchased at some craft stores. Use bead-head pins with this project because they are easy to find and remove. Regular straight pins are hard to find in the terry fabric and could be a nasty surprise for someone hugging the doll.

Finished Size

12 in. (30 cm)

Time: Two to three hours

What You Need

Materials
- facecloth
- ¼ lb. (125 g) or less of stuffing
- matching thread
- 4 rubber bands
- 12 x 6 in. (30 x 15 cm) broadcloth, for face
- yarn, for hair
- 2 eyes (see pages 6 and 7)
- wooden Popsicle stick
- craft glue
- 2 yds. (2 m) satin ribbon, ¼ in. (.5 cm) wide

Tools
- scissors
- ruler and pen
- heavy book
- bead-head pins
- sewing needle
- paper

Words that you don't understand? See the Glossary at the back of the book.

1 BODY: Cut or peel any tags off the facecloth. Lay the facecloth flat, wrong-side-up. Measure and mark a line across the center of the facecloth.

Measure and divide the line into thirds, marking them.

2 Cut along your line from each side of the facecloth to your marks. Do not cut the center portion.

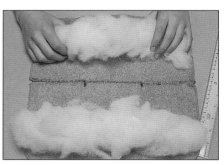

3 Form two sausage-shaped rows of stuffing, the length of the facecloth and about 3 in. (7.5 cm) wide. Lay them along the uncut sides of the facecloth.

4 Roll one side tightly (with the stuffing inside) to the center. Place a heavy book on top of the roll to keep it from unrolling.
Repeat with the other side. Pin the two rolls together.

5 Using a ladder stitch, sew the middle third of the rolls together. Tie off.

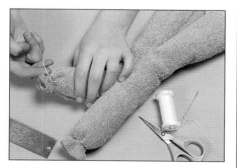

6 HANDS: Wind rubber bands around the ends of two rolls that are side-by-side, ½ in. (1 cm) from the ends. Remove any stuffing from the ends.

7 FEET: Wind rubber bands around the ends of the two remaining rolls 1½ in. (4 cm) from the ends.
Fill one foot with stuffing. Squeeze the end shut and sew it closed along the edge. Repeat for the remaining foot.

8 Stitch the cut edges down along the arms and legs, sewing them to the rolls. For an extra neat job, turn the cut edge under as you go. Tie off. This is the back of the doll.

9 Bend the arms down. Pin along the creases to hold them in place. Sew the creases closed on the front and back of the doll. Be sure to remove all pins.

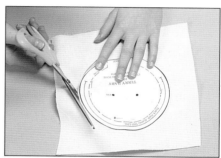

10 HEAD: Trace or photocopy the HEAD pattern on page 14 onto paper and cut it out. Pin it to two layers of broadcloth and cut along the solid line. Set the head pieces aside.

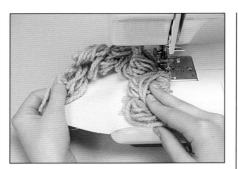

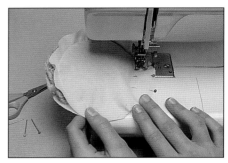

11 Cut a piece of yarn about 18 in. (46 cm) long. This is for tying. Set it aside for the moment.

Using the remaining yarn, make a bundle of yarn by looping it around your fingers about ten times. Slip the end of the tying-yarn through the loops and tie it. Make seven bundles, and tie them in a row on the yarn, all 1½ in. (4 cm) apart.

12 Place the string of bundles on the right side of one head piece with the tied edges inside the seam allowance. (See pattern for placement.) Pin and baste the bundles in place, inside the seam allowance. Remove the pins.

13 Place the head pieces with right sides together. (The yarn should be between the two pieces.) Pin well. With a ½ in. (1 cm) seam allowance, sew around the head, leaving the neck edge open. Remove the pins.

WAIT! DON'T CUT THIS PAGE!
If you cut out this pattern, you will destroy important information on the back of this page. Instead of cutting, trace or photocopy the pattern onto a sheet of paper.

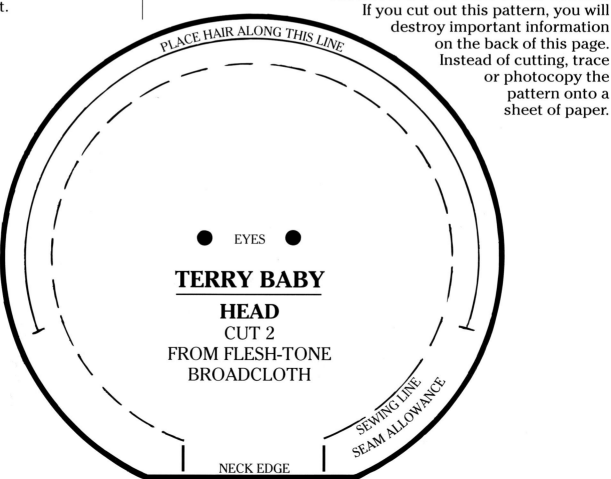

PLACE HAIR ALONG THIS LINE

● EYES ●

TERRY BABY

HEAD
CUT 2
FROM FLESH-TONE
BROADCLOTH

SEWING LINE
SEAM ALLOWANCE

NECK EDGE

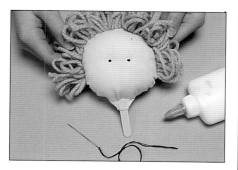

14 Turn the head right-side-out and attach the eyes. See pattern for placement. (Read about eyes on pages 6 and 7.) Fill the head with stuffing.

Push the Popsicle stick into the center of the head through the neck opening so that 2 in. (5 cm) is sticking out. Glue it in place. Allow the glue to dry.

15 Trim the ends of the hair.
Place the head in position on the body, with the face to the front and the Popsicle stick in the crease at the top of the body. Using a ladder stitch, sew the head securely to the body.

Tie ribbons tightly around the ankles and wrists, gluing or sewing them in place. Remove the rubber bands.

16 *Optional:* If you wish to make Terry Baby sit up, bend the legs up to the front, pin and stitch across the creases. Remove all pins.

Snow Baby

Snow Baby looks like a little kid in a snowsuit with a pom-pom on his hat. Make this loveable little toy from a soft, new sock. The heel of the sock becomes his cute little butt. This doll needs only a small amount of sewing, either by hand or by machine.

Finished Size

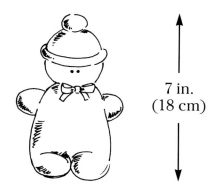

7 in. (18 cm)

Time: Two to three hours

Words that you don't understand? See the Glossary at the back of the book.

What You Need

Materials
• ladies size, cotton sock
• matching thread
• 3 handfuls of stuffing
• 2 eyes (see pages 6 and 7)

Tools
• paper and pencil
• scissors
• ruler or tape measure
• a few pins
• sewing needle

Optional
• craft glue
• pom-pom, for hat
• 18 in. (45 cm) ribbon

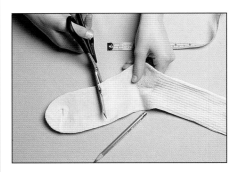

1 Trace or photocopy the patterns pieces on this page onto paper. Cut out the patterns.

Lay the sock flat on its side. Measure and mark 4 in. (10 cm) from the heel toward the toe. Cut across the sock at the mark. Save the sock's toe and set it aside.

2 Turn the sock wrong-side-out. Flatten the front.

3 LEGS: Pin the LEGS pattern onto the flat sock, with the curved ends of the legs at the cut edge of the sock. Cut along the solid line.

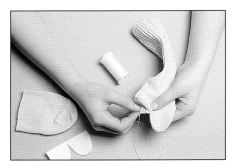

4 Pin the legs. Sew by hand or machine, near the edge.

5 BODY: Turn the sock right-side-out.

Measure and mark halfway from the heel to the top of the sock. This will be the neck. Fill with stuffing up to the mark.

Sew a running stitch around the sock at the mark. Pull the stitching tight to gather it. Tie off your sewing.

6 HEAD: Measure and mark halfway from the neck to the top of the sock. Fill with stuffing to the mark. Sew around the sock at the mark and gather tightly. Tie off.

Fold the ribbing down to create the hat. There will be a small hole at the center of the hat. Don't worry. This will be covered later with a pom-pom.

WAIT! DON'T CUT THIS PAGE!

If you cut out these patterns, you will destroy important information on the back of this page. Instead of cutting, trace the pattern onto a sheet of paper.

SNOW BABY

LEGS

CUT AS SHOWN, STEP 3

SNOW BABY

ARMS

CUT 4

7 ARMS: Find the toe that you cut off the sock. Turn it wrong-side-out and flatten it. It will be two layers.

Pin the ARMS pattern to the two layers of toe and cut it out. Do the same thing for the second arm.

8 Pin the arms and sew around the curved edges. Do not sew the straight sides closed.

9 Turn one arm section right-side-out. Fill it with stuffing. Turn the open edges in and sew them closed using ladder stitch. Repeat for the other arm.

10 Pin one arm to each side of the body. The straight edge of the arm should be against the body.

Sew the arms in place using a ladder stitch.

11 *Optional:* Instead of using a pom-pom, make a round ball for the top of Snow Baby's hat. Using the leftover toe of the sock, cut a circle about 2 in. (5 cm) across. Sew and gather around the edge. Stuff the ball, as you pull the gathers tight. Tie off.

12 Glue or stitch the pom-pom or the ball to the center-top of the hat. Allow it to dry. Tie a ribbon around Snow Baby's neck, if you wish.

13 Sew, paint or glue eyes onto the face. (Read about eyes on pages 6 and 7.)

Seasonal Sensations

A Collection of Ornaments

These three ornaments brighten the fall and winter seasons. Two traditional but very different angels are welcome in any home and they make glorious gifts for the holidays. The Folk Art Angel is stylized and looks her best when she's made from richly colored fabrics, twigs, braid and natural decorations. The romantic Paper Angel is a blur of pastel ribbon and a soft rustle of paper and lace.

And for Halloween, our little witch haunts a party casting a smile-spell on everyone – even the scariest of Halloween trick-or-treaters.

These ornaments are fast and fun to make and they're not expensive. If you are making several ornaments for gifts or for a bazaar, make them faster by collecting all of your materials first. Then, instead of making one complete ornament at a time, work in assembly-line style, doing each step for all of the ornaments.

Top left: Folk Art Angel, page 20. Bottom left: Wacky Witch, page 25. Above: Paper Angel, page 23.

How to do it

Folk Art Angel

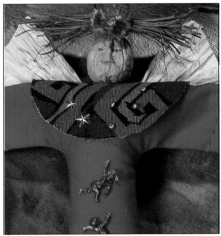

Part of the fun of making a Folk Art Angel is hunting for your own carefully selected twigs, leaves and dried flowers. Sew her from richly colored and textured fabric. Then add bits of lace, braid, beads or buttons. The sewing on this angel goes quickly and can be done by hand or by machine.

Finished Size

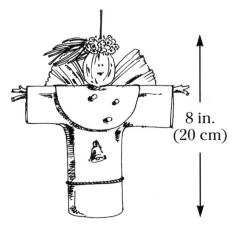

8 in. (20 cm)

Time: Two hours, plus drying time

What You Need

Materials
- 9 x 16 in. (23 x 40 cm) fabric, for body
- 5 in. (13 cm) square of fabric, for cape
- matching thread
- stuffing
- 1 or 2 twigs for arms, 10 in. (25 cm) long
- craft glue
- walnut, for head
- masking tape
- string or heavy thread
- raffia, yarn or dried flowers, for hair
- 8 in. (20 cm) twisted paper ribbon, for wings
- permanent markers or acrylic paint and a small brush

Tools
- paper and pen
- scissors
- pins
- sewing needle
- ruler

Optional
- buttons, braid, lace, feathers, etc. to decorate

Words that you don't understand? See the Glossary at the back of the book.

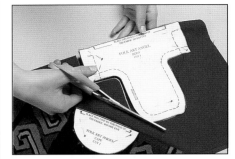

1 BODY: Trace or photocopy the patterns on page 22 onto paper. Cut out the patterns.

Fold the body piece of fabric in half. Pin the BODY pattern to the fabric with the top edge on the fold. Cut along the solid line but don't cut the fold.

Cut out the CAPE the same way.

2 Fold the body piece in half along the fold line with right sides together. Pin the edge.

Starting at the edge of one sleeve, sew a ½ in. (1 cm) seam around the body and out to the edge of the other sleeve. Clip the underarms and notch the curve.

Turn out the body through a sleeve hole.

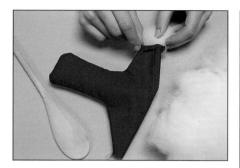

3 Fill the body to the top with stuffing, through an arm hole. Do not fill the arms; they stay empty.

4 Starting at the end of one sleeve, slip the twig(s) through and out the other sleeve, pushing the stuffing down if needed.

5 Hand stitch across the sleeves about ½ in. (1 cm) from the ends.
Apply glue to the center-top and center-front of the body. Center the cape over the top of the body. Pin it in place.

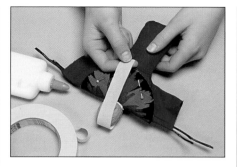

6 HEAD: Glue the wide end of the walnut onto the center-top of the body. Be generous with your glue. Tape the head securely in place. Allow the glue to dry. Remove all pins.

7 HAIR: Tie an 18 in. (46 cm) piece of string or heavy thread around a bunch of small dried flowers, knotted raffia or yarn.
Glue the bunch in place on top of the angel's head. Tape in place. Allow the glue to dry.
Knot the ends of the string to make a loop for hanging your angel.

8 WINGS: Cut two small slits in the back of the cape.
Cut two pieces of paper ribbon 4 in. (10 cm) long. Untwist one end of each. Place the twisted end into the slit. Glue and tape them in place, adding feathers or other decorations if you wish. Allow the glue to dry and remove the tape.

9 FINISHING: Glue or sew any braid, buttons, lace or other decorations onto the angel.
Using permanent markers or acrylic paints and a small brush, paint or draw a face on the front of the walnut.

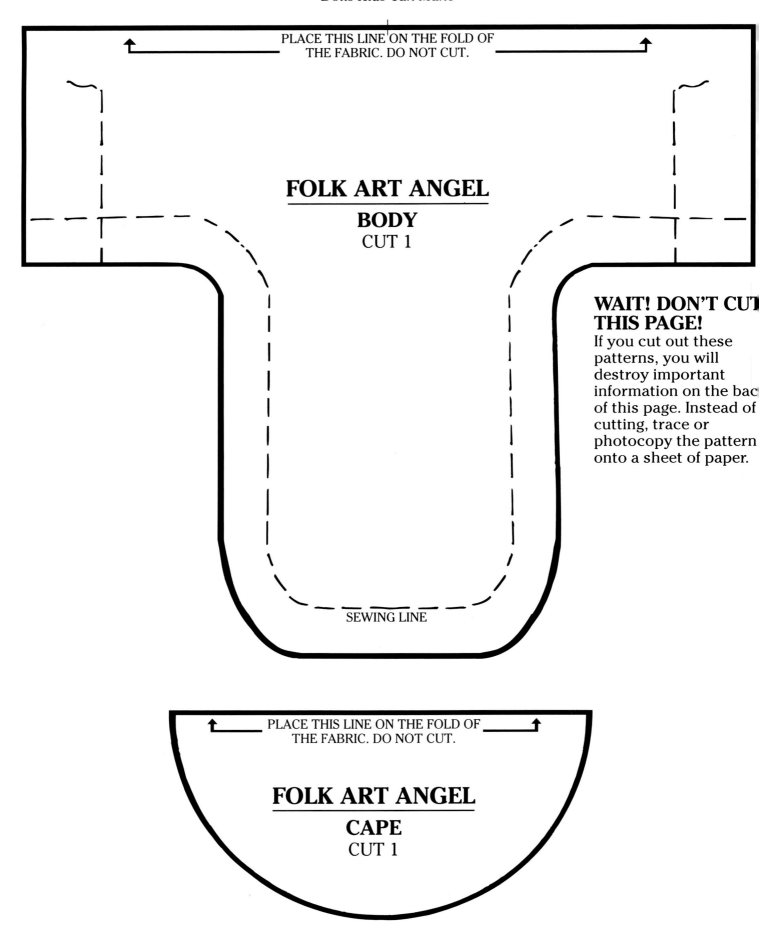

PLACE THIS LINE ON THE FOLD OF
THE FABRIC. DO NOT CUT.

FOLK ART ANGEL
BODY
CUT 1

WAIT! DON'T CUT THIS PAGE!
If you cut out these patterns, you will destroy important information on the back of this page. Instead of cutting, trace or photocopy the pattern onto a sheet of paper.

SEWING LINE

PLACE THIS LINE ON THE FOLD OF
THE FABRIC. DO NOT CUT.

FOLK ART ANGEL
CAPE
CUT 1

Paper Angel

Made from pieces of twisted paper ribbon and some lace for wings, Paper Angel can be made quickly, just by folding and tying, then gluing on her wings and head. There is almost no sewing on this angel. When she's finished, she can either hang from the tree or she can go on top. She also makes a lovely table ornament.

Finished Size

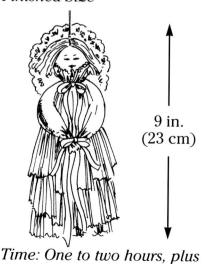

9 in. (23 cm)

Time: One to two hours, plus drying time

What You Need

Materials
- 2¼ yd. (2 m) twisted paper ribbon
- rubber band
- 1½ yd. (1.5 m) satin ribbon, ⅜ in. (1 cm) wide
- craft glue
- 2 facial tissues
- 12 in. (30 cm) of lace, 2 in. (5 cm) wide
- matching thread
- yarn or rope, for hair
- masking tape
- styrofoam ball, 1½ in. (4 cm) in diameter
- heavy thread

Tools
- warm iron
- ruler
- scissors
- sewing needle and a long darning needle
- pins

Optional
- permanent markers or acrylic paint and a small brush
- pliers

Words that you don't understand? See the Glossary at the back of the book.

1 BODY: Ask an adult to supervise while you use the iron. Turn on the iron to a low setting.

Cut ten pieces of twisted paper ribbon in various lengths from 6 to 8 in. (15 to 20 cm).

Untwist the paper ribbon and iron it. It should be flat with a crinkly texture.

2 Crunching one end of each strip, bundle the long strips, lining up the crunched ends. Then add shorter and shorter ones around the outside.

3 Wind a rubber band around the crunched ends, about 1½ in. (4 cm) from the end.

Cut a 30 in. (76 cm) piece of the satin ribbon and tie a bow around the neck, hiding the rubber band, or remove the rubber band if you wish. Glue the ribbon in place.

4 ARMS: Lift one paper ribbon strip on the side of the body. Measure and cut it to 4½ in. (11.5 cm). Place a crunched facial tissue against the underside. Fold one edge of the strip over the tissue. Then fold the other edge over so that the tissue is captured inside. Twist the end of the strip.

5 Repeat step 4 with another strip on the opposite side of the body.

Bend the two arms to the center of the front of the body, crossing them at the "wrists". Tie a piece of satin ribbon in a bow around the wrists gluing the bow in place.

6 WINGS: Using the 12 in. (30 cm) piece of wide lace, fold the lace in half so that it is now 6 in. (15 cm) long. Baste the two layers together close to one edge and gather tightly. Tie off.

7 Open the wings. Place them on the angel's back with the seam running from the top of the collar, down over the neck-ribbon. Glue the wings in place. Pin them if necessary and allow the glue to dry. Remove the pins.

8 HEAD: Cut ten pieces of yarn or rope, each 6 in. (15 cm) long. Lay them side-by-side. Cut a piece of masking tape 6 in. (15 cm) long. Lay the sticky side of the tape across the center of the yarn pieces. The ends of the tape will hang over.

Wacky Witch

9 Turn the hair over with the tape attached. Squeeze a line of glue across the center of the yarn pieces. Glue the yarn onto the styrofoam ball, taping it in place. Allow the glue to dry. Then remove the tape. Fray the ends of the yarn if you wish.

11 Using a large darning needle and heavy thread, doubled and knotted, push the needle through the styrofoam ball from the center-bottom through the center-top. You may need pliers for this job. Cut the thread 10 in. (25 cm) from the top of the head. Tie the ends of the thread in a knot.

Our pudgy, high flying, funny-faced witch is made from a knee-hi stocking, some black fabric and felt. No two witches will look the same. They are all different and each has her own funny personality.

Finished Size

10 *Optional:* Paint or draw a face onto the front of the styrofoam ball. Allow to dry.

12 Spread the collar open and glue the head in position, keeping the hair free. Be generous with your glue. To hold the head in place, insert two or three pins through the collar into the head. Make sure that the head is set well down into the collar. Allow the glue to dry thoroughly. Remove the pins.

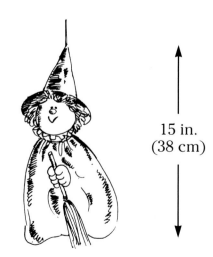

15 in. (38 cm)

Time: Two to three hours

What You Need

This whole project can be sewn by hand. However, you may prefer to use a sewing machine for steps 12 and 13.

Materials
• sandalfoot knee-hi stocking
• 5 handfuls of stuffing
• rubber band
• beige and black thread
• red heavy thread or embroidery thread
• raffia or straw for broom
• twig, 5 in. (13 cm) long, for broomstick
• craft glue
• masking tape
• black felt square
• plastic bag
• piece of black T-shirt knit, 8 in. x 18 in. (20 x 46 cm)
• gray yarn, for hair
• 2 eyes (see pages 6 and 7)
• blusher

Tools
• ruler
• scissors
• darning needle
• sewing needle
• pen or pencil
• paper
• pins

Words you don't understand? See the Glossary at the back of the book.

1 NOSE: Place a small blob of stuffing inside the knee-hi stocking, 1½ in. (4 cm) from the toe seam. On the outside of the knee-hi, wind a rubber band around the blob of stuffing, so that it makes a round ball about ½ in. (1 cm) across.

Tightly wind beige thread around the nose, just in front of the rubber band. Pull it tight and tie a tight knot. Remove the rubber band.

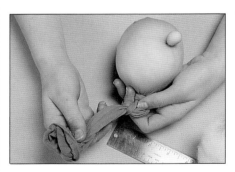

2 HEAD: Fill the toe-end of the knee-hi with stuffing and squish it to form a ball, about 2½ in. (6.5 cm) wide by 3½ (9 cm) long, with the nose in the center. Tie a knot in the knee-hi at the "neck".

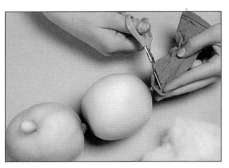

3 BODY: Stuff the knee-hi some more to make another ball about the size of the head. Tie another knot at the bottom of the ball. Cut off the excess knee-hi and set it aside.

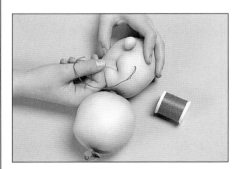

4 MOUTH: Thread the darning needle with the red embroidery thread and knot it twice. Push the needle through the back of the head, coming out the front half-way between the nose and the neck knot. Make a large stitch to form the left side of a "V", pushing the needle out through the back of the head. Pull tight and tie off.

Repeat this step, making the right side of the "V" shape. (The knots at the back of the head will be covered by a hat.)

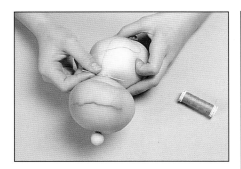

5 Tip the body ball up, towards the back of the head. Sew the body to the head.

6 HANDS: Find the left-over piece of knee-hi and cut two pieces 2 x 2½ in. (5 x 6.5 cm). Using one piece, fold it in half, along its length.

Start sewing a running stitch at the fold. Sew across one end and along the length. Stop sewing, but don't cut the thread. Fill the tube with stuffing. Continue sewing across the remaining end.

Pull the thread and gather the seam tightly. Tie off.

Repeat for the second hand.

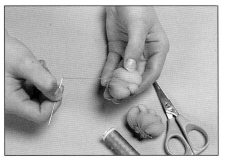

7 FINGERS: Sew four large stitches through the hand, pulling them tight. Tie off.

Repeat for the second hand. Sew the gathered edges of the hands together.

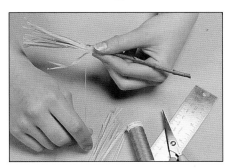

8 BROOM: Cut 20 pieces of raffia or straw, 3 in. (7.5 cm) long. Wind some thread around one end of the twig. Continue winding, catching the pieces of raffia in the thread. Tie off.

9 Glue the broom between your witch's hands. Tape the hands together around the broom and allow the glue to dry. Remove the tape.

10 HAT: Trace or photocopy the pattern pieces on page 29 onto paper and cut them out. Pin them to the black felt and cut one PEAK and one BRIM.

Fold the peak into a cone shape with the flap overlapping the opposite straight edge. Sew or glue the flap in place. If gluing, secure with tape.

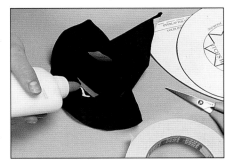

11 Squeeze glue onto each point on the inside edge of the brim. Place the peak onto the brim. Fold the glued points up onto the inside edge of the peak and tape them in place.

Stuff the hat with a plastic grocery bag (the glue won't stick to the bag) to hold the points in place. Allow the glue to dry and remove the tape and the bag.

12 DRESS: Cut a piece of black T-shirt knit fabric, 8 x 18 in. (20 x 46 cm). Fold it in half across its width, with right sides together. Pin. Using black thread, sew the side seam. Turn it right-side-out.

13 Baste around the top, ½ in. (1 cm) from the edge. Slip the dress onto Wacky Witch with the basted edge around the neck. Gather the basting until it fits snuggly around the neck. Tie off the gathering securely. Tack the dress to the neck in several places.

14 HAIR: Cut a piece of yarn, 18 in. (46 cm) long. This is for tying. Make a bundle of yarn by looping it around your fingers ten times. Slip the end of the yarn through the loops and tie it near the end. Make six bundles and tie them in a row on the yarn, all 1 in. (2.5 cm) apart.

15 Place the hat onto the witch's head. Draw a line around it, where it touches her head.
Tie the ends of the row of bundles together. Place the circle of bundles of yarn on the witch's head just above the line. Adjust to fit if necessary. Stitch in place.

16 Put some stuffing into the hat. Then cover the witch's bald head with her hat, pulling it part way over the the yarn bundles. Sew in place.
Cut the bundles of yarn to make strands of hair and trim the yarn as needed.

17 Sew the hands to the front of the body using a ladder stitch, sewing through the dress and body material. To hang up the witch, slip a length of thread through the point of the hat and knot the ends.
Sew, paint or glue the eyes onto the face. (Read about eyes on pages 6 and 7.)
Dust Wacky Witch's cheeks, nose and hands with blusher.

↑ PLACE THIS
LINE ON FOLD ↑

↑ PLACE THIS
LINE ON FOLD ↑

FOLDLINE

WITCH'S HAT
BRIM
CUT 1 BLACK FELT

WAIT! DON'T CUT THIS PAGE!
If you cut out these patterns, you will
destroy important information on the
back of this page. Instead of cutting,
trace or photocopy the patterns onto
a sheet of paper.

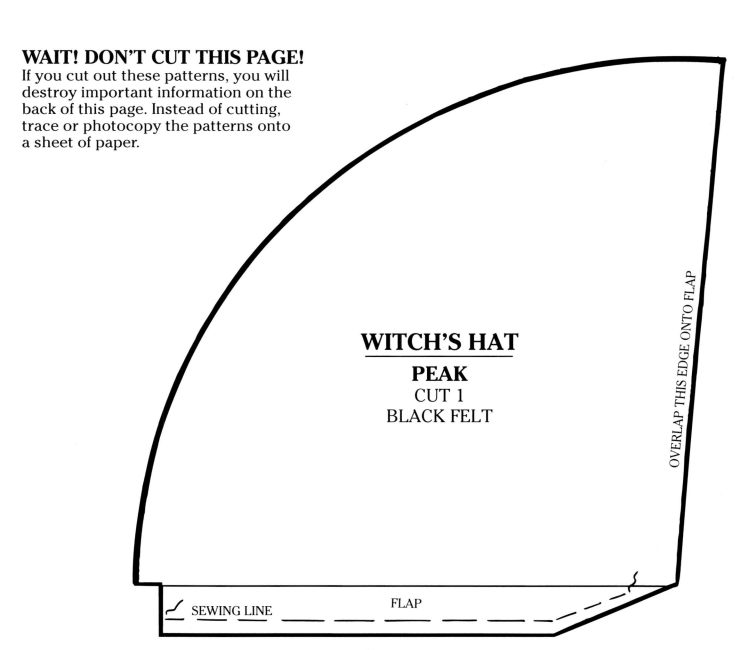

OVERLAP THIS EDGE ONTO FLAP

WITCH'S HAT
PEAK
CUT 1
BLACK FELT

SEWING LINE   FLAP

Heaven Scent

A Lacy Potpourri Doll

Like a hovering guardian angel, this ornamental doll made from lace and potpourri hangs on the wall, adding a sweet scent to any room – kitchen, bath or bedroom. Imagine the surprise and delight when she's given as a gift. And although she's so attractive, she's not at all expensive or difficult to make.

If you want to keep the cost of making this potpourri doll low, try substituting tulle (the mesh that a ballerina's tutu is made from) for the wide lace. Cut it to size and decorate with lace strips that you may have left from another project.

How to do it

What You Need

Choose lace with a tight weave. The whole doll can easily be sewn by hand. However, you may wish to use a sewing machine for steps 6 and 7.

Materials
- styrofoam ball, 2 in. (5 cm) diameter
- 3 in. (7.5 cm) square of panti-hose
- craft glue
- synthetic doll hair
- 44 in. (110 cm) lace, about 5 in. (12.5 cm) wide
- 1 yd. (1 m) gathered lace, 1 in. (2.5 cm) wide
- matching thread
- 1 yd. (1 m) very narrow ribbon or cord
- 2 oz. (60 g) potpourri (small pieces only)
- 4 rubber bands
- 2 yd. (2 m) satin ribbon, ⅜ in. (1 cm) wide

Tools
- scissors
- ruler
- pins
- sewing needle
- large bowl
- paper
- very fine crochet hook or loop-turner

Finished Size

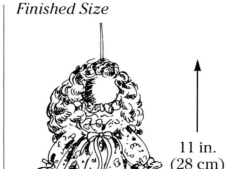

11 in. (28 cm)

Time: Two to three hours

Words that you don't understand? See the Glossary at the back of the book.

1 HEAD: Using the point of your scissors, make a hole about 1 in. (2.5 cm) deep in the styrofoam ball. This will be the top of the head.

Stretch the panti-hose square over the ball. Squeezing some glue into the hole, push the ends of the panti-hose into the hole.

2 Bundle together the synthetic doll hair (about half the package). It is not necessary to find cut ends.

Using a strand of hair, wind it around the bundle close to the end. Squeeze more glue into the hole and push the end of the hair into it.

3 Lift the hair. Apply glue to the head and arrange the hair onto the glue. Don't worry if the hair is all different lengths or if there are bald spots. These can be fixed later.

Allow the glue to dry, while you make the body.

4 Remove the cat from doll-making materials.

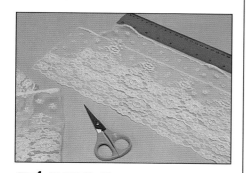

5 BODY: For arms, cut one piece of wide lace, 12 in. (30 cm) long.
For legs, cut another piece, 16 in. (40 cm) long. Set aside the remaining piece.

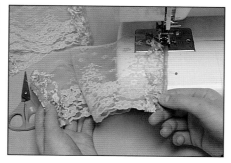

6 Measure the width of the wide lace. Cut four lengths of gathered lace matching the measurement.
With right sides together, place the edge of one piece of gathered lace onto one cut edge of an arms piece. Pin. Sew a narrow seam.
Repeat for the remaining three ends of the arms and legs.

7 Fold one piece of lace in half along its length with the right sides together. Pin. Sew a narrow seam along the full length, including the lace at the ends.
Repeat for the second piece. Turn out the arms and legs.

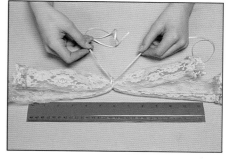

8 Flatten both lace tubes. Place the shorter piece (the arms), centered on top of the longer piece (the legs). Place both seams together.
Using the very narrow ribbon or cord, tie it around the arms and legs at their center point, measuring if necessary. Tie a very tight square knot. Do not trim the ribbon.

If you can't find the ribbon...

9 Pour the potpourri into a large bowl.

Roll up a sheet of paper. Place it into the end of one arm. Fill the arm with potpourri. When the arm is filled, remove the paper and wind a rubber band tightly around the "wrist".

Repeat for the other arm and the legs.

Working over a large piece of clean paper makes for easier clean-up.

10 One by one, remove the rubber bands and tie satin ribbon tightly around the wrists and ankles, covering the seam lines.

To ensure the ribbons don't come undone, squeeze a drop of glue under the bow as you tie it.

11 Check the ends of the doll's arms and legs to be sure they are closed tightly. If not, glue a small scrap of fabric into the end to prevent potpourri from falling out.

Stand the doll up and crunch her arms and legs so that the potpourri settles.

12 SKIRT: Find the remaining piece of wide lace. It should be 16 in. (40 cm) long. Fold it in half with the right sides together, matching the cut ends. Pin. Sew a narrow seam across the cut ends. Turn out the skirt.

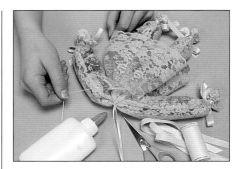

13 Starting at the seam, baste around the top edge of the skirt, about 1 in. (2.5 cm) from the edge.

Slip the skirt onto the doll with the seam at the center-back. Gather the basting to fit the doll, placing the gathers about 1 in. (2.5 cm) below her underarms. Tie off.

Tie satin ribbon tightly around the gathers. Glue it in place.

14 COLLAR: Fold the leftover piece of gathered lace, about 15 in. (38 cm) long, in half, matching the cut ends. Baste the gathered edge through both layers. Gather the edge tightly.

Join the folded end to the cut ends to make a circle. Tack together at the center. Tie off.

15 Slip the very narrow ribbon through the center of the collar. Tack the center of the collar to the body.

Check the doll's head. Trim the hair to the desired length. But watch out! Cut the hair a little longer than you want it to be. It tends to "shrink"! Glue or sew extra pieces into any bald spots. Allow the glue to dry.

16 Place the doll's head on the body and mark the center-top and center-bottom of her head with pins.

Remove the head and, starting at the center-top of her head, insert the very fine crochet hook or loop-turner through the hair and into the styrofoam, bringing it out at the center-bottom. Remove the pins.

17 Hook onto the very narrow ribbon and draw it through the head, being careful not to damage the panti-hose or the hair. If necessary, cut a small hole in the panti-hose at the center-bottom to draw the hook back through.

18 Squeeze some glue onto the center of the collar. Then push the head along the ribbon so that it is firmly against the collar. Using the ribbon that goes through the head, tie a bow against the head, gluing it in place. Allow the glue to dry.

19 Tie a knot at the ends of the very narrow ribbon and hang up the doll.

Great Grannies!

A Traditional Mop Doll

Grannies come in all shapes and personalities. There are Grannies that bake pies and cookies, knit mitts, paint the house and pump their own gas. Then there are Grannies that paint abstract art, work in the garden, travel the world, and sail boats. And there are also Grannies who cook gourmet dishes, play with their grandchildren, and read murder mysteries. Grannies are fascinating people.

Our Granny is a mop doll, a traditional doll that has been updated so that she is easy to make. The first mop doll was probably invented long ago by an old-fashioned Granny. Perhaps she wanted to make a doll for her grandchild's birthday with the materials she had handy: some scraps of fabric and a mophead.

This old-fashioned Granny Doll makes you feel cozy just looking at her. And that's a nice feeling.

How to do it

What You Need

You may wish to use a sewing machine for steps 9 and 10.

Materials
- large rope mophead
- craft glue
- rubber bands
- sandalfoot knee-hi stocking
- 3 large handfuls of stuffing
- matching thread
- 30 x 12 in. (75 x 30 cm) broadcloth, for dress
- 8 in. (20 cm) wide gathered lace, for shawl
- 30 in. (75 cm) satin ribbon, ¼ in. (.5 cm) wide, for shawl
- 2 eyes (see pages 6 and 7)
- felt square for bonnet
- 1 yd. (1 m) narrow gathered lace for bonnet
- masking tape

Tools
- scissors
- ruler
- darning and sewing needles
- pins
- iron
- pencil
- compass

Optional
- novelty glasses
- basket and/or bunch of flowers
- blusher and make-up brush

Finished Size

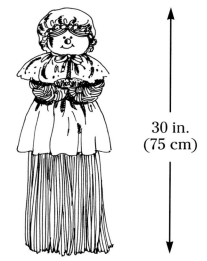

30 in. (75 cm)

Time: Three to four hours

Words that you don't know? See the Glossary at the back of the book.

1 BODY: Lay the mophead flat. Cover the woven center strip as follows. (This will be the front of your doll.) At the top of the woven strip, lift six strands of rope on each side, 12 strands in total.

Divide the 12 strands into three bunches, each bunch with four strands.

2 Braid the bunches loosely until the braid is the length of the woven center strip. Tie string (snip a strand from the mop) around the end of the braid.

Glue the braid onto the woven strip. Allow the glue to dry. This is the front of the doll.

3 ARMS: At the top of the braid, lift 51 strands of rope on one side. Divide into three bunches of 17 strands each. Braid.

Wind two rubber bands around the braid, 6½ and 8 in. (16 and 20 cm) from the start. Cut across the braid between the rubber bands. Save the bundled cut-off piece to be used later as hair for Granny.

Repeat for the second arm. Tie a strand (snipped from the mop) tightly around each wrist and remove the rubber bands.

4 Bend the arms, bringing them together at the center of the front, 2 in. (5 cm) below the top. (If you want Granny to carry a basket, slip it onto her arm now.) Glue the wrists to the body. Allow the glue to dry.

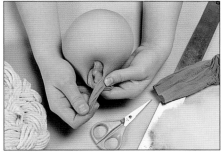

5 HEAD: Before you start, file any rough spots on your fingernails to prevent snags on Granny's face.

Measure and cut a 6 in. (15 cm) piece from the toe of a knee-hi. Fill it with stuffing, until it is 4½ in. (11 cm) across. Tie the open end shut. This will be the neck.

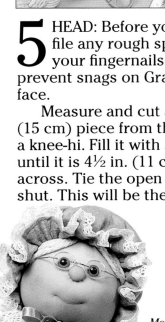

6 NOSE: Use a darning needle, threaded double and knotted, for all sewing on the face.

Hand sew a circle about 1 in. (2.5 cm) across, in the center of the face. Use medium-sized stitches. Pull the stitches tight to gather, making sure that there is stuffing in the nose. Tie off and cut the thread.

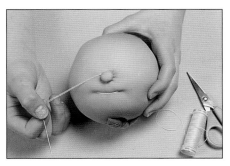

7 MOUTH: Push the needle into the top of the nose, coming out halfway between the nose and the chin. Make a big stitch, about 1½ in. (4 cm) across. Bring the needle back out at the top of the nose. Pull it very tight. Tie off and cut the thread.

Most mopheads have a chemical smell. This smell will usually disappear when the mop is aired for a few days.

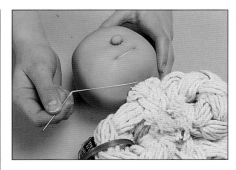

8 Sew the head to the body. Position the head with the knot centered on top of the braid and the face toward the front. Sew tightly, using a ladder stitch, 1 in. (2.5 cm) from the knot, pulling the stitches tight. If you sew too close to the knot Granny will have a wobbly head. Don't worry if your stitching is messy. It will be covered by the shawl.

9 DRESS: Fold the dress piece in half across its width with right sides together. Pin and sew the side seam. Press the seam open.

Hem the top and bottom edges. Turn them over twice, ¼ in. (.5 cm) to the wrong side. Press, pin and sew the edges. Remove all pins.

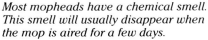

10 Turn out the dress. Baste around the top edge below the hem. Slip the dress onto the doll so that the top edge is under the arms. Gather the basting to fit Granny. Tie off. Tack the top of the dress in place.

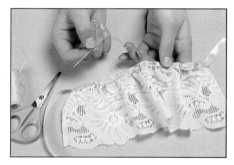

11 SHAWL: Fold under and stitch the cut edges of the wide gathered lace.

Center the gathered edge of the lace onto the ribbon. Pin. Sew. Tie the shawl around Granny's neck. Tack in place.

12 EYES: Glue, paint or sew eyes onto Granny's face. (Read about eyes on pages 6 and 7.) If Granny will be wearing glasses, try the glasses on for size and then position the eyes. Remove the glasses and attach the eyes.

13 BONNET: Using a compass, draw a circle 11 in. (28 cm) across onto the felt square. Cut out the circle. Sew the narrow gathered lace around the top edge of the circle.

Baste around the circle, about 1 in. (2.5 cm) from the edge. Gather the basting, sizing the bonnet to Granny's head. Tie off. Set aside.

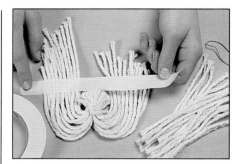

14 HAIR: Count 30 strands in one bundle of rope that you cut from the arms. Keep the rubber band on the bundle and pull out the rest of the strands. Tie a strand tightly around the bundle behind the rubber band. Remove the rubber band.

Part the strands in the middle. Bend the strands to make a W shape. Lay a piece of tape across the ends of your hair.

15 Place the bonnet on Granny's head. Draw a line on her head, close to the gathered edge of the bonnet. Remove the bonnet.

Position the hair so that the ends will be under the bonnet, taping them in place. Lifting the hair carefully, squeeze glue under it. Smooth the hair down. Allow the glue to dry. Then remove the tape.

16 *Optional* BUN: Find the second bundle of rope cut from the arms. Tie a strand tightly around the bundle in front of the rubber band. Remove the rubber band.

Hold the bundle up-side-down like a fountain. Smooth the loose ends over the bundled end and tie them together. Stitch the tied end of the bun under the edge of the bonnet.

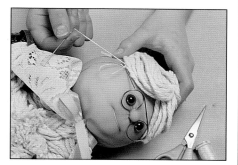

17 *Optional* GLASSES: Glue or stitch novelty glasses in place.

18 *Optional* CHEEKS: Using a large make-up brush, lightly dust Granny's cheeks and lips with blusher.

19 *Optional* FLOWERS OR BASKET: Stitch or glue flowers to Granny's hands or into her basket.

20 Position the bonnet on Granny's head, with the bun (if you made one) at the center-back of the head. The bonnet should cover all cut ends of hair as well as your drawn line. Stitch the bonnet in place.

FORGET THAT ROCKING CHAIR DEARIE!

Sporty Granny's T-shirt and shorts are made like the Cool Dudes! (See page 48.) Her tights are made from knee-hi's. The shoes and socks are baby-sized. You may need to trim some rope from the mop to fit the clothes.

Baby, Baby, Oh Baby!

A Life-sized Newborn Baby Doll

Create a work of modern art with this funny, cuddly Baby. Everyone loves her button nose and silly little Mona Lisa smile. Using a real baby sleeper makes her a realistic size. Get the smallest sleeper with feet that you can find, one that will fit a newborn. A used or discount sleeper is fine for Baby.

Baby's head, hands and body are all made from panti-hose. The body, which is inside the sleeper and won't be seen, can be made from a used pair, while the head and hands should be made from a new pair. For the new panti-hose, try to get a large or queen-sized pair that has a sheer toe, rather than a reinforced toe. Remember the color becomes much lighter when the panti-hose is stretched. It's a good idea to file your nails before you start to work on Baby. Otherwise there might be some snags on Baby's face.

How to do it

What You Need

Materials
- new pair of sandalfoot panti-hose, for head and hands
- 1 lb. (500 g) white polyester stuffing
- rubber bands
- heavy thread to match panti-hose
- 2 eyes (see pages 6 and 7)
- 3 in. (8 cm) square of fake fur, for hair
- small baby sleeper (newborn size)
- thread to match collar and cuffs of sleeper
- used pair of panti-hose, for body

Tools
- scissors
- ruler
- darning needle
- pins

Optional
- craft glue
- blusher and make-up brush

Finished Size

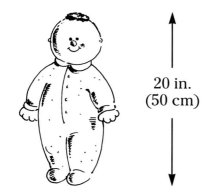

20 in. (50 cm)

Time: Three to four hours

Words that you don't know? See the Glossary at the back of the book.

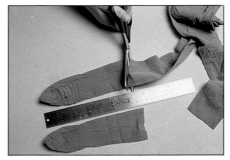

1 ARMS: Measure from one toe of the new panti-hose and cut a piece 7 in. (18 cm) long. Do this again with the other toe end. The toe ends will become the baby's hands.

2 Fill the arms halfway with stuffing. Wind a rubber band around the panti-hose, close to the stuffing. Tie thread next to the rubber band. These are the elbows. The stuffed half should be plump and round.

Fill the tops of the arms with stuffing. Tie the ends shut using a square knot.

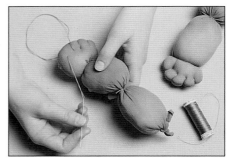

3 Make a wrist. Wind a rubber band around the arm about 1½ in. (4 cm) from the end. Then tie thread tightly behind the rubber band. Repeat for the second arm. Remove the rubber bands.

To make fingers, use a darning needle and thread and sew four very big stitches on one hand, pulling each stitch tight. Tie off. Do this again with the other hand. Set the arms aside.

4 HEAD: Measure and cut a length of new panti-hose, 7 in. (18 cm) long. Tie one end shut using a square knot. Turn the head inside-out, so that the knot is inside. This is the top of the head.

Form a ball of stuffing as big as a melon. Push the stuffing into the panti-hose and tie the open end shut. It should be firm. This knot will be the neck. The head should be about 5 to 5½ in. (12 to 14 cm) across.

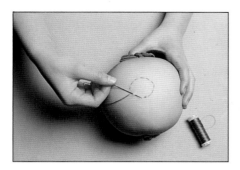

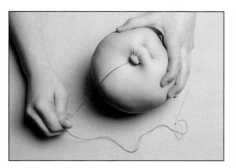

5 NOSE: Use a darning needle, threaded double with heavy thread and knotted, for all sewing steps that create the face.

To make the nose, sew a circle about 1½ in. (4 cm) across, just below the center of the head. Use medium-sized stitches. Pull the stitches tight to gather, checking that there is stuffing in the nose.

Tie off, but don't cut the thread.

7 MOUTH: Push the needle into the top of the nose, coming out halfway between the nose and the bottom knot. Make a huge stitch, about 1½ in. (4 cm) across. Bring the needle back out at the top of the nose. Pull it very tight. Tie off and cut the thread.

9 EYES: Sew, paint or glue eyes onto the face. (Read about eyes on pages 6 and 7.)

10 HAIR: Cut a circle of fake fur 2½ in. (6.5 cm) across. Cover Baby's knot and give her hair by gluing or stitching the piece of fake fur over the knot.

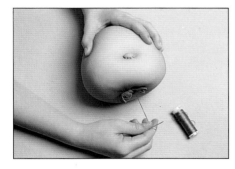

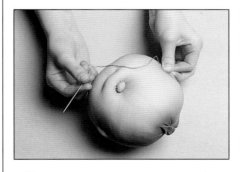

6 CHEEKS: Push the needle through the top of the nose and out through the knot at the neck. Pull it very tight. Tie off and cut the thread.

You may think the face looks pretty strange, but don't give up. It improves with every step.

8 EARS: Grab a pinch of panti-hose on one side of the head. Stitch it tightly and tie off. Repeat for the other ear. They should be level with the nose.

11 With the sleeper closed, pin the head in place. Using thread that matches the neck of the sleeper, sew on the head. Set your fat-headed, droopy baby body aside.

12 BODY: For this you will need the top of the used panti-hose with its legs attached.

Measure down from the crotch 7 in. (18 cm) on both legs and cut the panti-hose.

Tie thread around each leg at the crotch.

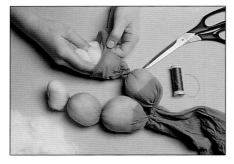

13 Fill each leg half full with stuffing. Tie thread around each leg at the end of the stuffing. These will be Baby's knees.

Fill each leg two-thirds full of stuffing. Tie thread around each leg again. These will be the ankles.

Fill the end of the legs with stuffing. Tie them securely shut. These are the feet.

14 Stuff the top of the panti-hose, so that it is plump and squishy. This will be Baby's chest.

Roll the waistband of the panti-hose over and sew it down. It will form "tabs" at the ends for attaching the arms. Baby's body is certainly strange looking, but remember, it won't be seen.

15 Sew the knots at the ends of the arms to the "tabs" on the body.

16 Open the sleeper and put the body inside. The hands should stick out of the sleeves and the feet should be in the feet of the sleeper.

Sew the head to the top of the body, sewing at least 1 in. (2.5 cm) away from the knot. If you sew any closer, Baby's head will be wobbly.

Make a strong stitch through the bottoms of the feet and into the panti-hose, so that the feet won't pull out.

Sew all openings in the sleeper shut, so that Baby won't undress herself.

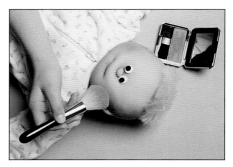

17 *Optional:* To give your Baby rosy cheeks and lips, brush on some blusher.

Give Baby a hug!

Cool Dudes

A Modern Rag Doll

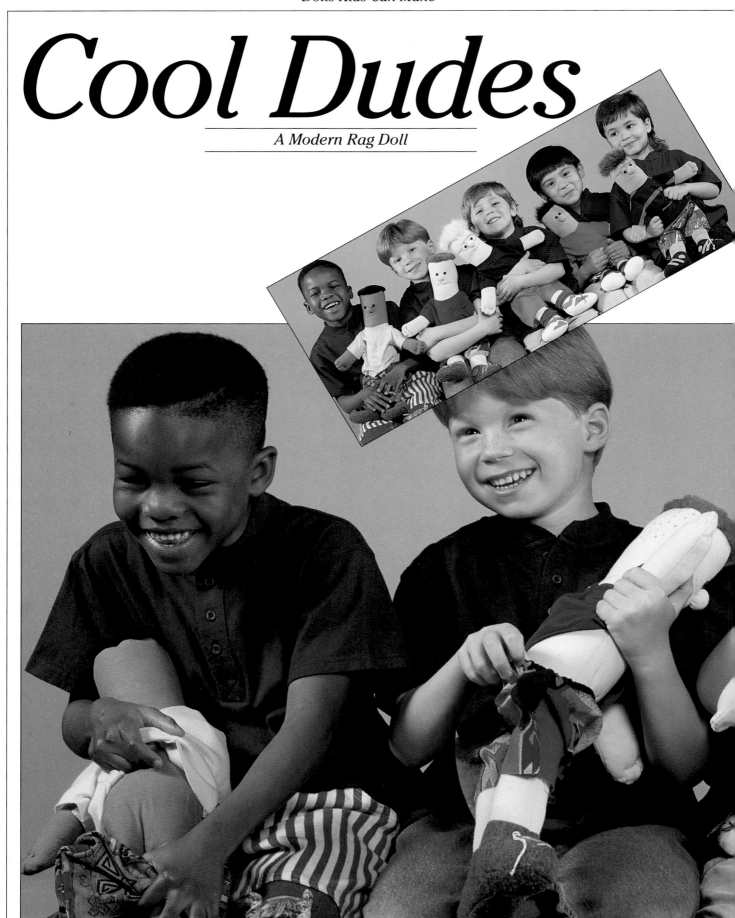

When you think of rag dolls, forget those raggedy characters Anne and Andy. Instead, think of these cool dudes. Then make some to look like kids you know!

Rag dolls have always been handmade dolls – a collection of bits and pieces of fabric, yarn, paint and decorations. This is what makes a rag doll unique, one-of-a-kind. And it's no different for these hip hop guys. You can cut the T-shirt from one of your favorite old ones, add an earring or two, draw on some stubble around his high-top-fade, glue on a watch, bend and attach wire glasses or layer a grunge look on your doll. It's all up to your own imagination.

How to do it

What You Need

This project is best sewn on a machine. Make sure there is an adult around to supervise. Some hand sewing is also required. All fabrics, except the fake fur, are at least 28 in. (70 cm) wide. T-shirt knit fabric is best for the body. However, if you use a woven fabric, sew a narrow ¼ in. (.5 cm) seam allowance.

Materials
- ½ yd. (.5 m) flesh-tone T-shirt knit, for body
- ⅓ yd. (.3 m) broadcloth, for shorts
- ⅓ yd. (.3 m) T-shirt knit, for shirt
- ¼ yd. (.25 m) sweatshirt knit, for sneakers
- 5 in. (13 cm) square fake fur, for hair
- thread to match body
- ½ lb. (250 g) stuffing
- 6 in. (15 cm) narrow elastic
- 2 eyes (see pages 6 and 7)

Tools
- pen, paper (or photocopier)
- scissors
- tape
- pins
- iron
- sewing needle

Optional
- safety pin
- fabric paints, markers, felt, jewelry, novelty glasses, hat, toy watch
- craft glue

Time: Four to five hours

Words that you don't know? See the Glossary at the back of the book.

CUTTING LAYOUT

 PINK is the right side of the fabric.

 YELLOW is the wrong side of the fabric.

- 8 PATTERN PIECES

FLESH-TONE T-SHIRT KNIT

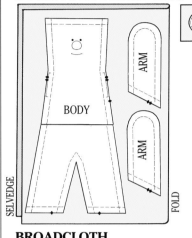

BODY

ARM

ARM

SELVEDGE

FOLD

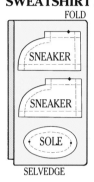 NOSE

SWEATSHIRT KNIT

FOLD

SNEAKER

SNEAKER

SOLE

SELVEDGE

T-SHIRT KNIT

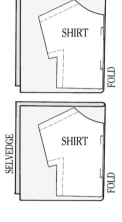

SHIRT

SHIRT

SELVEDGE

FOLD

FOLD

BROADCLOTH

SHORTS

SHORTS

FOLD

FOLD

FAKE FUR

HAIR

FOLD

CUTTING

- Trace or photocopy the pattern pieces onto paper. Following the Cutting Layout, pin the pattern pieces to the fabrics. Be sure that all pins are inside the cutting line.
- When cutting two pieces, fold the fabric with right sides together.
- When cutting a knit, place the stretch arrows in the direction of the fabric's stretch.
- Cut on the solid line, cutting all notches outward.
- Use sharp scissors for cutting.

SEWING

- Place fabric pieces with right sides together, unless otherwise specified.
- Pin fabric pieces with the pins crossing the sewing line. Sew over the pins.
- Use a medium-sized stitch and sew all seams ½ in. (1 cm) wide, unless otherwise stated.
- Sew along the broken line as indicated on the pattern.
- For different types of hand sewing stitches, see the Glossary at the back of the book.

Finished Size

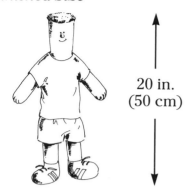

20 in.
(50 cm)

1 Trace or photocopy the pattern pieces on pages 54 through 57 onto paper. Following the Cutting Layout on page 50, cut out the patterns.

2 BODY: Place the ankle of one SNEAKER piece onto an ankle of one BODY piece, with right sides together matching the notches. Sew across the ankle. Press the seam open.
    Repeat for the remaining three ankles.

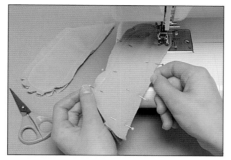

3 Place two ARM pieces with right sides together. Sew around the arm, leaving the notched side open. Repeat with the two remaining arm pieces. Notch the curves. Turn the arms right-side-out and fill them with stuffing.

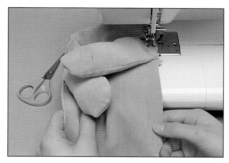

4 Flatten the open ends of the arms and baste them closed. Pin the arm pieces onto one body piece, matching the double notches.
    Baste the arms to the body inside the seam allowance.

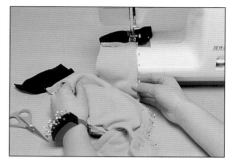

5 Place the two body pieces with right sides together and the arms inside.
    One side of the body has single notches. Pin that side, including the top of the sneaker. Sew, leaving the space between the notches open for turning and stuffing.
    Pin and sew the other side of the body.
    Clip the corners on the sneakers.

6 Sew the inside of the legs including the heels of the sneakers, pivoting at the crotch. Clip the V of the crotch.

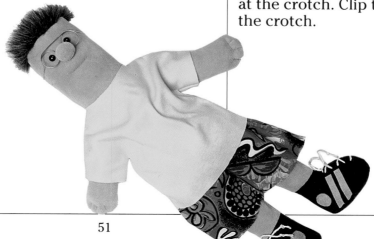

7 With the doll's body wrong-side-out, place the circle of HAIR into the top of the head, so that the right sides are together. (You should be looking at the wrong side of the fake fur.) Pin well. Sew a narrow seam ¼ in. (.5 cm) around the edge. This is easiest if the presser-foot of your machine is inside the head.

8 With the doll still wrong-side-out, place one SOLE piece into the bottom of one sneaker, matching the dots on the pattern to the seams. Pin well.

Sew around the edge by hand or by machine. This is easiest if the presser-foot is inside the sneaker. Repeat for the second sneaker and sole.

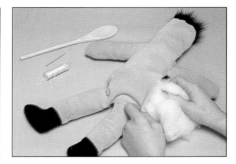

9 Turn the doll right-side-out through the side-body opening. Fill the doll with stuffing, making sure to get some into the sneakers. Hand sew the opening shut, using a ladder stitch.

10 CLOTHES: Place the two SHORTS pieces, right sides together. Sew the side seams. Sew the crotch, pivoting at the V. Don't sew across the leg openings or the waist. Clip the V at the crotch and the corners at the waist.

11 Fold the top edge to the wrong side ¼ in. (.5 cm) and iron it. Fold again ½ in. (1 cm). Iron again. Sew close to the fold-edge, leaving about 1 in. (2.5 cm) open.

Thread the elastic through the waist. (Attaching a safety pin to the end of the elastic helps to feed it through.)

Secure the elastic with a few stitches and hand sew the opening shut.

Fray the leg openings, or finish them by turning and sewing the edge under.

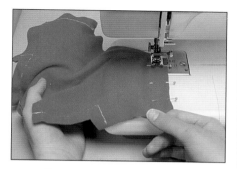

12 Place the two SHIRT pieces, right sides together. Pin and sew the sides and underarms, pivoting at the corners. Pin and sew the shoulders. Don't sew across the neck or arm openings.

Clip the corners at the armpits. Press the seams open. Turn out. Dress your Cool Dude.

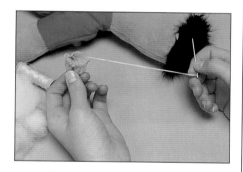

13 FACE: Hand sew small running stitches close to the edge of the NOSE piece. Gather the stitching tightly, stuffing the nose as you gather. Tie off.

Sew the nose to the face using a ladder stitch. (See pattern for placement.)

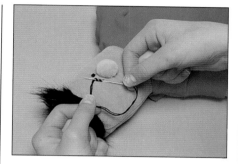

14 Sew, paint or glue on the eyes. (Read about eyes on pages 6 and 7.) (See pattern for placement.)

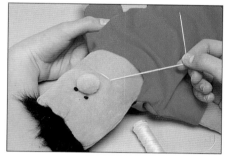

15 Make the mouth by painting it on with fabric paints or permanent markers, or by sewing a very large stitch and pulling it tight. (See pattern for placement.)

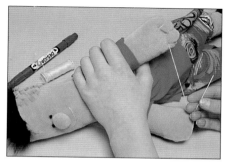

16 *Optional:* Make fingers by sewing three large stitches in each hand, pulling them tight. Draw on stubble around his high top fade with a felt marker. You can glue felt stripes onto the sneakers. Or add an earring.

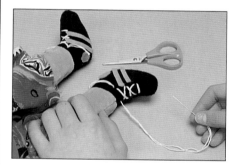

17 *Optional:* Try making shoe laces from string or dental floss. You can also add novelty glasses, a hat, necklace, toy watch, soft schoolbooks or a backpack made from felt.

WAIT! DON'T CUT THESE PAGES!

If you cut out these patterns, you will destroy important information on the backs of the pages. Instead of cutting, photocopy or trace the pattern onto a sheet of paper.

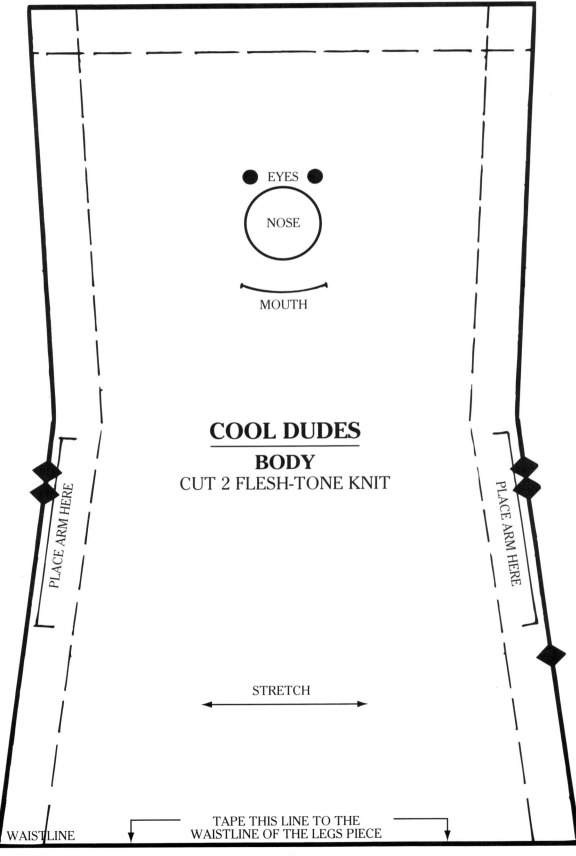

EYES

NOSE

MOUTH

COOL DUDES
BODY
CUT 2 FLESH-TONE KNIT

PLACE ARM HERE

PLACE ARM HERE

STRETCH

WAISTLINE

TAPE THIS LINE TO THE
WAISTLINE OF THE LEGS PIECE

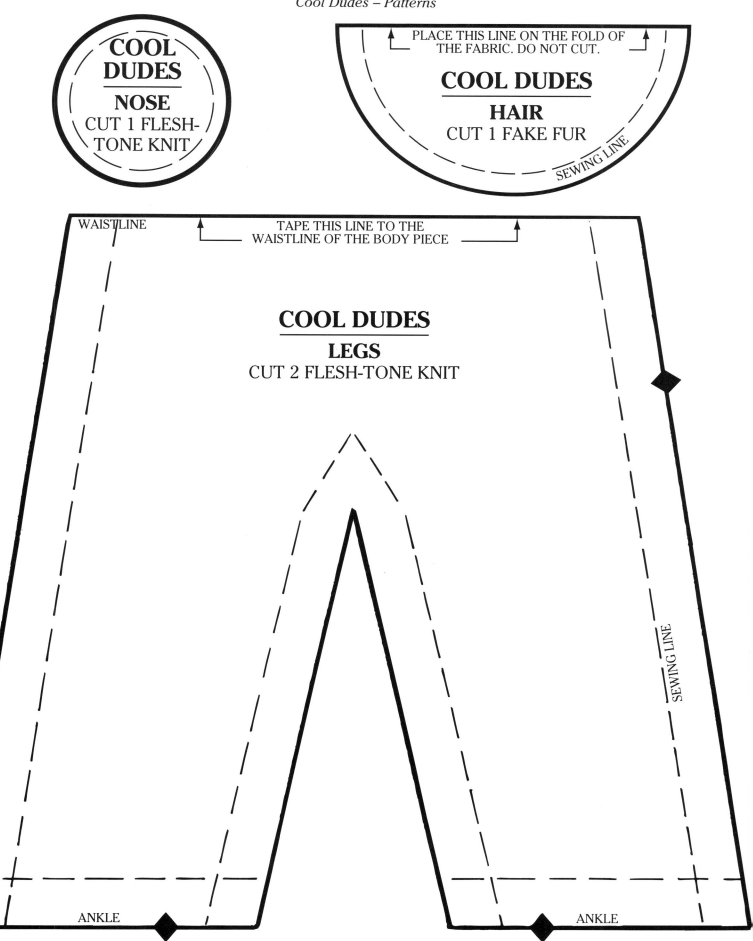

COOL
DUDES

NOSE
CUT 1 FLESH-
TONE KNIT

PLACE THIS LINE ON THE FOLD OF
THE FABRIC. DO NOT CUT.

COOL DUDES

HAIR
CUT 1 FAKE FUR

SEWING LINE

WAISTLINE

TAPE THIS LINE TO THE
WAISTLINE OF THE BODY PIECE

COOL DUDES

LEGS
CUT 2 FLESH-TONE KNIT

SEWING LINE

ANKLE

ANKLE

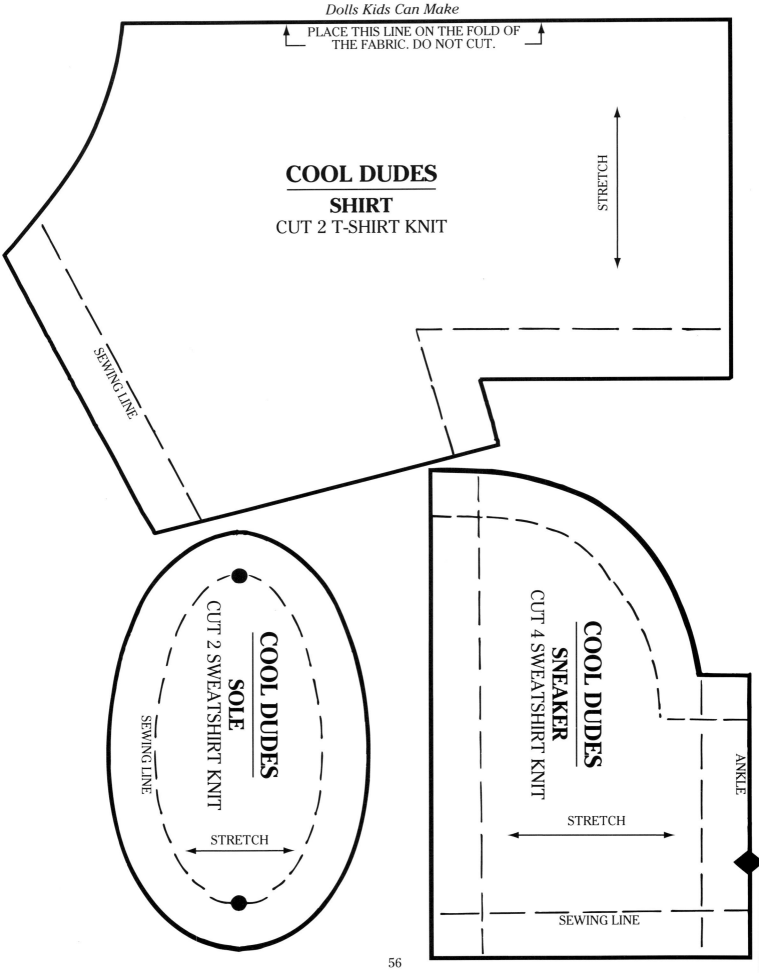

PLACE THIS LINE ON THE FOLD OF
THE FABRIC. DO NOT CUT.

STRETCH

COOL DUDES

SHIRT
CUT 2 T-SHIRT KNIT

SEWING LINE

COOL DUDES
SOLE
CUT 2 SWEATSHIRT KNIT

SEWING LINE

STRETCH

COOL DUDES
SNEAKER
CUT 4 SWEATSHIRT KNIT

STRETCH

ANKLE

SEWING LINE

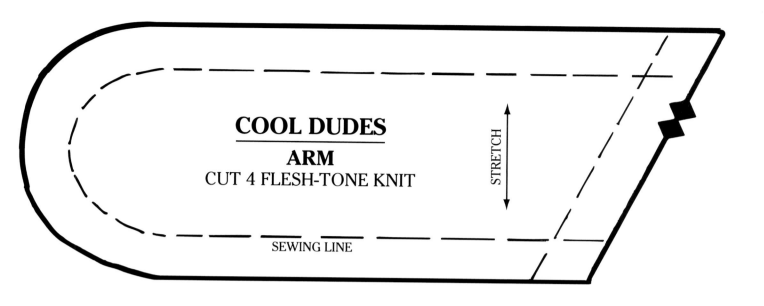

COOL DUDES

ARM

CUT 4 FLESH-TONE KNIT

STRETCH

SEWING LINE

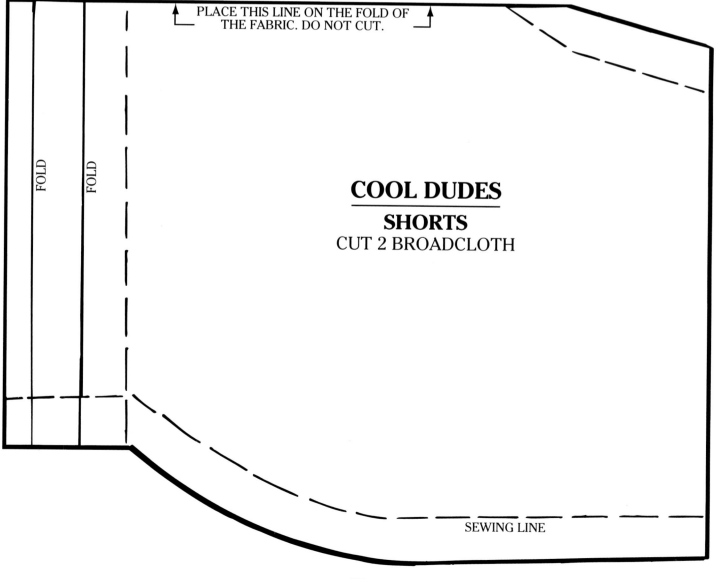

PLACE THIS LINE ON THE FOLD OF
THE FABRIC. DO NOT CUT.

FOLD

FOLD

COOL DUDES

SHORTS

CUT 2 BROADCLOTH

SEWING LINE

Once Upon a Time

A Double Doll

Make two dolls and a story all at once. On one side is Little Red Riding Hood, all dressed up in her best hood and cape, ready for her walk through the woods. Turn her upside down and it's Big Bad Wolf, dressed in Grandma's clothes and waiting to trick Red into becoming his dinner!

Everyone loves this Double Doll because it's a surprise as well as a great story-starter. While Red and Wolfie look fabulous, they are inexpensive to make, because most of the fabric pieces are small scraps. Use mainly red printed cottons for Little Red Riding Hood and granny-like fussy prints for the Big Bad Wolf. Then add some left-over lace and felt details to both characters.

You'll need a little experience on a sewing machine and some patience to make this doll. There are many small pieces to cut out and sew together and every step must be followed carefully for the doll to turn out properly.

In order not to be rushed, give yourself a weekend to assemble, cut and sew from start to finish.

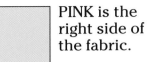

How to do it

What You Need

Sew this doll with a sewing machine. Be sure that there is an adult around to supervise the machine sewing and ironing.

Materials
- 2 lengths broadcloth (one red), each piece ½ yd. (.5 m), for 2 dresses
- 10 in. (25 cm) square flesh-tone broadcloth, for Red
- 12 in. (30 cm) square of gray knit, for Wolfie's head
- scrap of gray broadcloth, for Wolfie's hands
- 2 felt squares (one red), for Red's cape and Wolfie's bonnet
- scraps of felt: gray, pink, black, white
- thread (sew full doll with a light color)
- ¼ lb. (125 g) stuffing
- 1½ yd. (1.5 m) narrow lace, for bodice fronts and bonnet
- yarn, for Red's hair
- 4 eyes (see pages 6 and 7)
- 60 in. (150 cm) gathered lace, minimum 2 in. (5 cm) wide, for skirt and shawl
- 2 yd. (2 m) narrow satin ribbon, for shawl and cape

Tools
- pen, paper (or photocopier)
- scissors
- pins
- iron
- wooden spoon
- measuring tape or ruler
- sewing needle

Optional
- blusher, fake fur, acrylic paints and brush

CUTTING LAYOUT

 PINK is the right side of the fabric.

YELLOW is the wrong side of the fabric.

- 12 PATTERN PIECES

RED RIDING HOOD

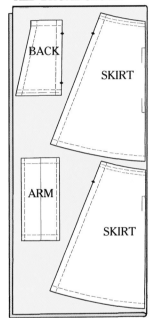

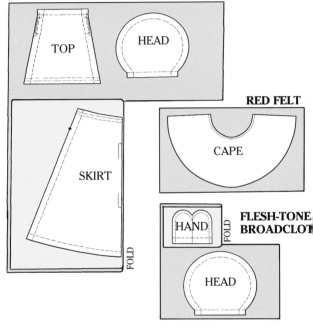

RED BROADCLOTH — BACK, SKIRT, ARM, SKIRT, SKIRT

RED BROADCLOTH — TOP, HEAD, SKIRT

RED FELT — CAPE

HAND — FLESH-TONE BROADCLOTH

HEAD

BIG BAD WOLF

 GRAY KNIT — SELVEDGE — WOLF'S HEAD — FOLD

 FELT — BONNET

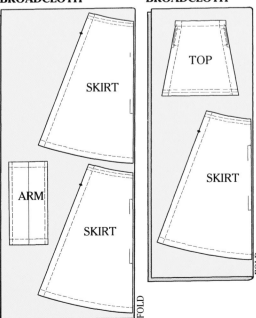 BROADCLOTH — SKIRT, ARM, SKIRT

BROADCLOTH — TOP, SKIRT

GRAY — EAR

PINK F. — EAR

GRAY BROADC. — HAND

 WHITE FELT — TOOTH

 BLACK FELT — NOSE

Finished Size

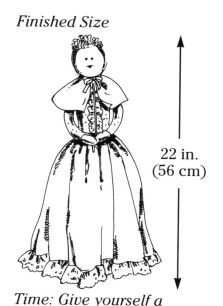

22 in.
(56 cm)

Time: Give yourself a weekend from start to finish

Words that you don't know? See the Glossary at the back of the book.

CUTTING

- Draw or photocopy the pattern pieces onto paper, enlarging them to 133%. Following the Cutting Layout, pin the pattern pieces to the fabrics. Be sure that all pins are inside the cutting line.
- When cutting two pieces, fold the fabric with right sides together.
- When cutting a knit, place the stretch arrows in the direction of the fabric's stretch.
- Cut on the solid line, cutting all notches outward.

SEWING

- Place fabric pieces with right sides together, unless otherwise specified.
- Pin fabric pieces with the pins crossing the sewing line. Sew over the pins.
- Use a medium-sized stitch and sew all seams ½ in. (1 cm) wide, unless otherwise stated.
- Sew along the broken line as indicated on the pattern.
- For different types of hand sewing stitches, see the Glossary at the back of the book.

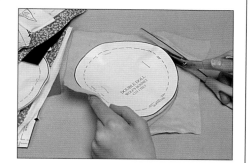

1 Photocopy the pattern pieces on pages 66 through 69 onto paper, to the sizes indicated on the pattern pages. Or, if you have a sewing grid with 1 in. (2.5 cm) squares, use it to draw the patterns, matching the squares on the patterns to the squares on the grid.

Following the Cutting Layout and the instructions, position and pin the pattern pieces on the fabrics. Cut them out. Keep some scraps about 3 in. (7.5 cm) square. You'll need them later to stuff the hands.

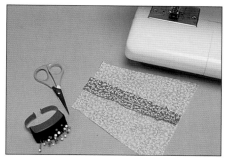

2 RED'S BODY: Place the two BACK pieces with right sides together, matching the notches. Pin. Sew from the notches to the ends leaving the center open. Press the seam open, including the middle unsewn area. Set this back piece aside.

3 Place the straight edge of one HAND piece onto the end of one ARM piece, with right sides together. Pin. Sew. Press the seam toward the hand.

Repeat with the remaining hand and arm.

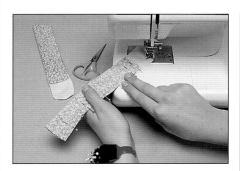

4 Fold one arm in half along its length, with right sides together. Pin. Sew a narrow seam, ¼ in. (.5 cm), along the side and around the end of the hand, ending at the folded edge. Repeat for the remaining arm.

Notch the curved edge and turn the arms right-side-out. The handle of a wooden spoon can help with turning out small and narrow articles.

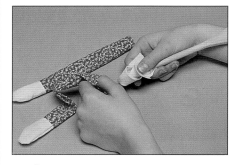

5 Fill the hands and arms with stuffing, or fill only the hands and let the arms stay limp. Do this by taking one of the fabric scraps that you saved, wrapping it around the end of the wooden spoon handle and pushing the scrap into the hand. Do both hands.

6 Cut two pieces of narrow lace, 6½ in. (16.5 cm) long. Center them, side by side, on the right side of the red TOP piece, running from the neck edge to the waist. Sew them in place with a straight or a zigzag stitch.

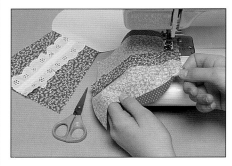

7 Place the flesh-tone HEAD piece onto the top piece with right sides together, matching the straight neck edge. Pin. Sew the straight, neck-edge seam. Press the seam open.

Repeat with the red head piece and the back piece.

(WOLF: Later, when you come back to do the wolf, lay one WOLF'S HEAD piece onto one TOP piece, right sides together, and sew the neck edge. Then repeat with the remaining wolf's head piece and top piece.)

8 Lay the front piece flat, right-side-up. Flatten the arms and place them onto the front piece with the raw edges together. (See pattern for placement.) Pin. Baste the arms in place inside the seam allowance.

9 RED'S HAIR: Make a bundle of yarn by looping it around your fingers about eight times. Remove and tie it together with another piece of yarn.

Make four to six bundles and lay them on the right side of the face, along the seam allowance at the center-top. (See pattern for placement.)

Pin in place and baste inside the seam allowance.

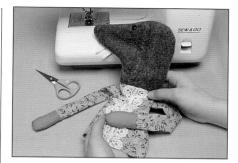

10 Place the front and back pieces, with right sides together, matching the neck seams. Pin well.

Starting at the waist, sew up the side, around the head and continue down to the waist. Do not sew across the waist. Notch the curved edge on the sides of the head. Turn out the body.

12 WOLF'S BODY: Position the two felt TOOTH pieces onto the right side of one WOLF'S HEAD piece and baste inside the seam allowance. (See pattern for placement.)

Repeat steps 3 through 11, skipping step 9, using the wolf's pattern pieces.

14 Place the edge of the wide gathered lace along the edge of the bottom of one skirt section with right sides together. Pin in place and baste near the edge. Cut off any excess lace and stitch the cut ends together.

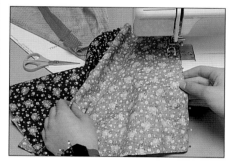

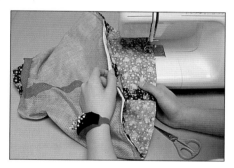

11 Attach the eyes. (Read about eyes on pages 6 and 7.) (See pattern for placement.) Set Red Riding Hood aside.

13 SKIRTS: Place two matching SKIRT panels, right sides together, matching notches. Pin and sew one side seam. Press the seam open.

Repeat twice, joining the three panels. You now have a cone-shaped skirt. The narrow edge of the cone is the waist and the wide edge is the bottom.

Repeat with the remaining three pieces. You now have two cones.

15 Place one skirt, which is wrong-side-out, over the other skirt, which is right-side-out. They should be right sides together, with the gathered lace inside. Match the seams and pin well around the bottom. Sew along the bottom catching the edge of the lace in the seam.

16 Turn the skirts right-side-out through the top opening. Pull on the lace to turn the sewn edge fully out and press well.

Match the waist edges, pinning at the seams. Baste around the top, close to the edge, with a large machine stitch.

17 Gather the basting until the top of the skirt fits Wolfie's waist. Evenly spread the gathers and tie off.

With the red side of the skirt facing out (and with the wolf's body turned right-side-out), slip the wolf inside the skirt, matching the wolf's waist to the gathers. Pin well around the gathered edge and baste with a narrow seam. When you flip the skirt down, it will match the wolf's clothing.

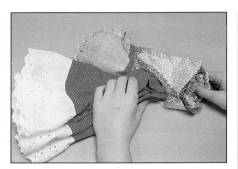

18 Now here's the tricky part. It may sound strange but just follow these instructions and you'll see that it works!

Turn Red Riding Hood wrong-side-out. Push her arms up into her head. Lay her down on her tummy.

Flip the skirt up over the wolf's head, so that the red skirt is showing. Slip the gathered waist edge of the skirt into the opening in Red's back. Push it in, until it is level with Red's waist. Check that the front of the wolf is lined up with the front of Red.

19 Pin the waist of Red to the gathered edge. Baste another narrow seam, then stitch the waist using the full seam allowance.

Turn Red right-side-out through the opening in her back.

20 Fill the doll with stuffing through the opening in Red's back. First stuff the wolf. The handle of a wooden spoon can help push stuffing into Wolfie's nose. Then stuff Red. Pin and hand stitch the opening closed, using a ladder stitch.

21 WOLF'S NOSE: Hand sew around the edge of the NOSE piece. Pull the thread to gather it into a ball, stuffing it as you gather it. Tie off.

Pin the nose to the point of the wolf's face and sew it to the face tightly, using a ladder stitch. (See pattern for placement.)

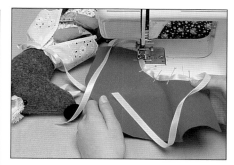

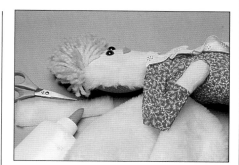

22
WOLF'S EARS: Place one of the pink and one of the gray felt EAR pieces together. Sew a very narrow seam around the edge. The ears do not get turned out.

Repeat for the second ear. Fold the ears in half lengthwise, with the pink inside. Pin and hand sew the ears to the sides of the head. (See pattern for placement.)

23
WOLF'S BONNET: Sew narrow lace around the top edge of the BONNET piece. Baste ½ in. (1 cm) from the edge. Gather the basting loosely. Position the hat on Wolfie's head and gather to fit. Tie off.

Cut two small slits where the ears are. Pull the ears through the slits. (See pattern for placement.)

24
WOLF'S SHAWL: Cut a piece of wide, gathered lace to fit around Wolfie's shoulders. Turn under and finish the cut ends.

Sew a length of narrow satin ribbon along the gathered edge, allowing 12 in. (30 cm) at each end for tying a bow. Tie around Wolfie's shoulders.

RED'S CAPE: Pin and sew narrow satin ribbon along the inside curve of the red felt CAPE piece, allowing 12 in. (30 cm) at each end for tying a bow. Tie the cape around Red's shoulders.

25
RED'S FACE: Trim Red's hair. Draw lips or sew on pink felt lips.

Brush blusher on Red's cheeks.

26
Optional: If you wish to make Red Riding Hood more glamorous, trim her hood with fur. Cut two narrow strips of fake fur and glue them over the seams on the sides of her head.

27
Optional: To create an old-fashioned hand painted face, prime the broadcloth with acrylic primer (gesso). Then paint a face over the primer with acrylic paints and a fine brush. You can make it detailed, as shown above, or more sketchy like Paper Angel, page 25.

The story of Little Red Riding Hood has changed from the original. In this book, printed in the 1930's, the wolf eats up both Granny and Red. In today's books, usually Granny hides in a closet while Red outwits the wolf and saves her.

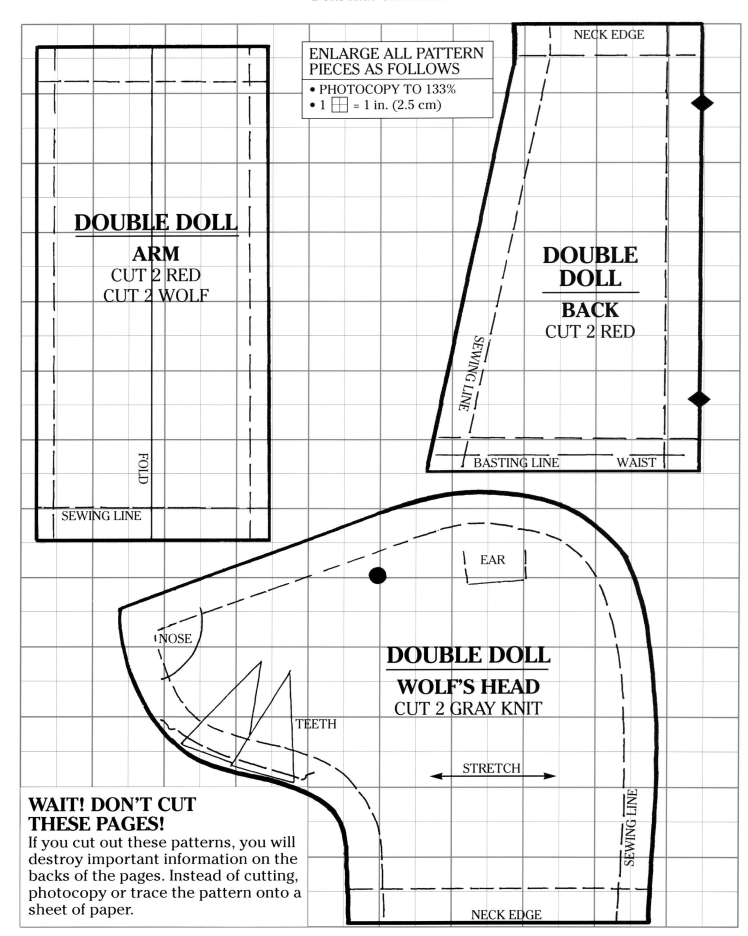

ENLARGE ALL PATTERN
PIECES AS FOLLOWS
- PHOTOCOPY TO 133%
- 1 ⊞ = 1 in. (2.5 cm)

NECK EDGE

**DOUBLE
DOLL**

BACK
CUT 2 RED

SEWING LINE

BASTING LINE   WAIST

DOUBLE DOLL

ARM
CUT 2 RED
CUT 2 WOLF

FOLD

SEWING LINE

EAR

NOSE

DOUBLE DOLL

WOLF'S HEAD

CUT 2 GRAY KNIT

TEETH

STRETCH

SEWING LINE

WAIT! DON'T CUT THESE PAGES!

If you cut out these patterns, you will destroy important information on the backs of the pages. Instead of cutting, photocopy or trace the pattern onto a sheet of paper.

NECK EDGE

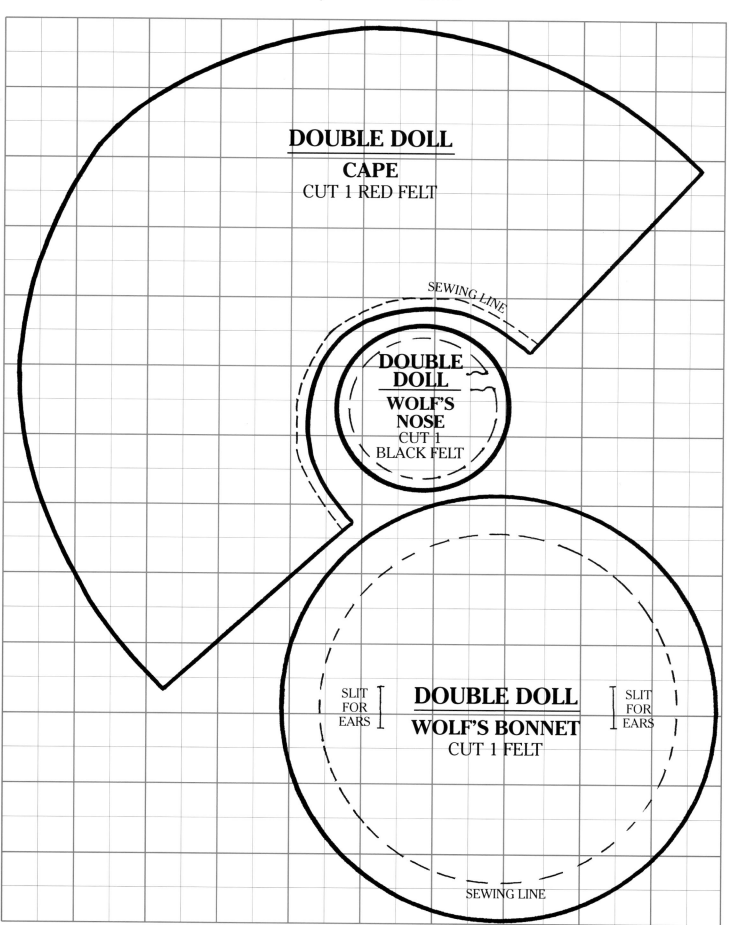

DOUBLE DOLL

CAPE
CUT 1 RED FELT

SEWING LINE

**DOUBLE
DOLL**

**WOLF'S
NOSE**
CUT 1
BLACK FELT

SLIT
FOR
EARS

DOUBLE DOLL

WOLF'S BONNET
CUT 1 FELT

SLIT
FOR
EARS

SEWING LINE

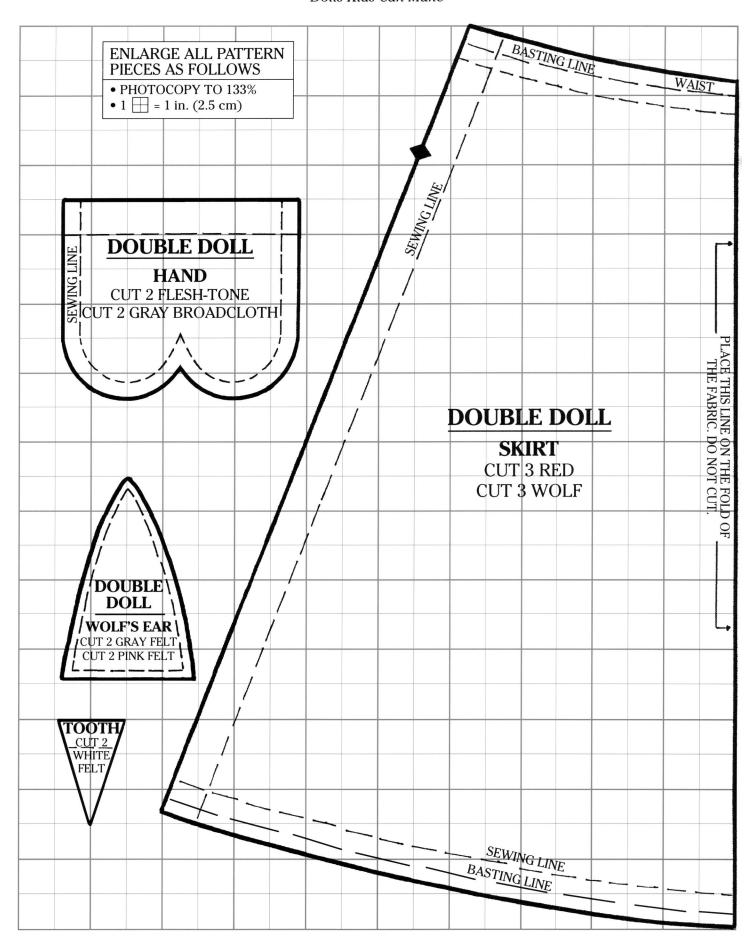

ENLARGE ALL PATTERN PIECES AS FOLLOWS
- PHOTOCOPY TO 133%
- 1 ⊞ = 1 in. (2.5 cm)

DOUBLE DOLL

HAND

CUT 2 FLESH-TONE

CUT 2 GRAY BROADCLOTH

SEWING LINE

DOUBLE DOLL

WOLF'S EAR

CUT 2 GRAY FELT

CUT 2 PINK FELT

TOOTH

CUT 2 WHITE FELT

BASTING LINE

WAIST

SEWING LINE

DOUBLE DOLL

SKIRT

CUT 3 RED

CUT 3 WOLF

PLACE THIS LINE ON THE FOLD OF THE FABRIC. DO NOT CUT.

SEWING LINE

BASTING LINE

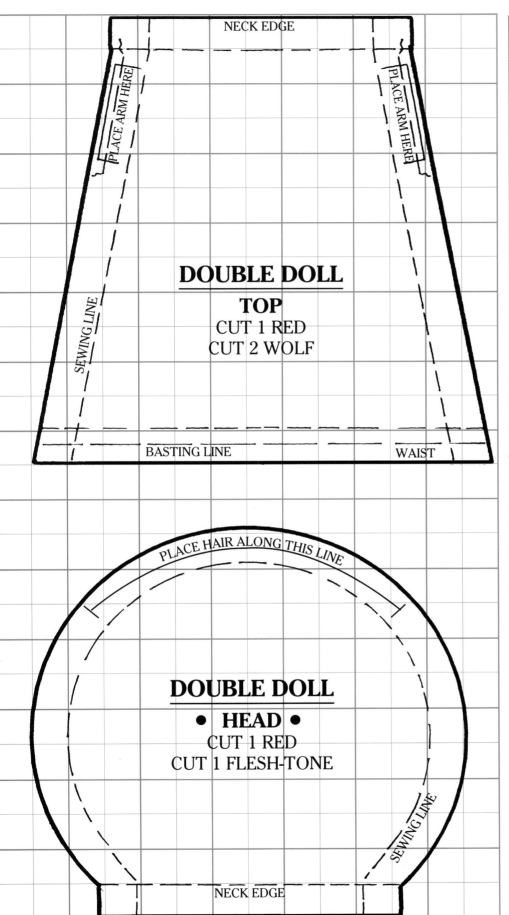

NECK EDGE

PLACE ARM HERE

PLACE ARM HERE

SEWING LINE

DOUBLE DOLL

TOP
CUT 1 RED
CUT 2 WOLF

BASTING LINE

WAIST

PLACE HAIR ALONG THIS LINE

DOUBLE DOLL

● HEAD ●
CUT 1 RED
CUT 1 FLESH-TONE

SEWING LINE

NECK EDGE

Red Riding Hood

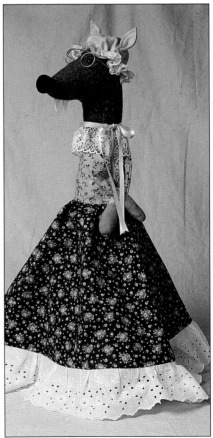

Big Bad Wolf

69

Glossary

SEWING AND CRAFT TERMS

baste – Large, loose stitches that help position fabric pieces for final stitching. Also used for gathering. By machine, use the largest stitch available on the machine. By hand, sew medium-sized running stitches.

braid – To make a braid, use three groups of yarn, joined at one end. Alternate lifting the side groups over the center group.

clip corner – To make a corner that is square when turned out, cut into the seam from the corner of the fabric to the pivot in the stitching. Do not cut stitching.

clip curve – To prevent puckering when an inward curve is turned out, cut into the seam allowance at regular intervals along the curve. Do not cut the stitching.

cutting line – The heavy, solid line on the patterns. Cut on the line.

diameter – The distance across the center of a circle.

dots – Black markings found on pattern pieces. These markings are to help position pattern pieces. The instructions will call for matching the dots to seams or other points.

French knot – An embroidery stitch that makes good doll's eyes. Use very heavy thread or light yarn. Follow the instructions below.

Pick up a tiny stitch next to the thread. Wind thread around point of needle three times.

Hold wound thread together and pull needle until tight. Draw needle through fabric close to the knot. Tie off.

gather – By machine, baste, then pull the bobbin thread, sliding the fabric along. Tie off.

By hand, sew medium-sized running stitches, then slide the fabric along the stitches. Tie off.

ladder stitch – An almost invisible stitch for sewing a seam on the right side. See diagram.

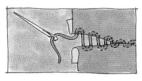

notch curve – To prevent bunching on an outward curve, cut V shapes (notches) at regular intervals along the curve, being careful not to cut the stitching.

notches – Black, diamond shaped markings found on the cutting lines of patterns. These markings are to help position pattern pieces. Cut notches outward. If you cut inward, you may make a hole on the seam.

◆◆ _____ ◆

DOUBLE NOTCH   SINGLE NOTCH

pivot – To turn a corner while machine sewing, lower the needle, lift the presser-foot and turn the fabric. Lower the foot and continue sewing.

running stitches – Basic, up-and-down hand sewn stitches in a line.

seam allowance – The distance between the cut edge of the fabric and the sewing line. Sew a ½ in. (1 cm) seam allowance unless otherwise stated.

selvedge – The factory finished edge of fabric.

sewing line – The broken line inside the pattern. Sew on this line. See seam allowance.

square knot – Also known as a reef knot. Tie first with the right ribbon over the left. Then tie with the left ribbon over the right. This knot won't slip open like a "granny" knot.

stuffing – Fill the hardest to reach places first, using the handle of a wooden spoon or a similar tool to push the stuffing. Use new, clean polyester fiber fill or cotton batting to fill your dolls.

stretch – Some pattern pieces have stretch arrows marked on them. Place the arrows in the direction of the stretch of the fabric.

tack – To anchor a fabric piece in place. Sew several stitches tightly in one spot. Then tie off.

thirds – Three equal sections.

tie off – To prevent stitching from opening. Draw the needle under the last stitch, then through the loop and pull tight as shown in diagram. Repeat two or more times.

turn out – To turn a sewn item right-side-out. To turn out a narrow long shape, use the handle of a wooden spoon or similar tool.

zigzag stitch – A sewing machine stitch that makes a zigzag pattern. Good for joining flat edges and for sewing stretch fabrics.

MATERIALS AND TOOLS

acrylic paints – Fast drying, water-based paints that are colorfast and waterproof and come in a huge array of premixed colors. Acrylic paints are good for painting on fabric.

broadcloth – A type of fabric weave that is stable, medium-light in weight and usually washable. Broadcloth can be a mix of many fiber types, such as cotton, polyester, rayon and silk.

compass – A V-shaped instrument used to draw circles. Hold the point in the center of the circle, adjust the width of the compass for the size of the circle desired and swivel the pencil to draw the circle.

craft eyes – Made from molded plastic with a post on the back, these eyes come with a grommet. They are available at craft stores. Attach as shown in diagrams below.

Craft eyes are plastic with a post on the back. Cut a very small hole on the right side of the doll's face. Push the post through.

On the wrong side, push the grommet all the way onto the post.

craft glue – A white glue available at art and craft stores. Craft glue dries clear. White carpenter's glue can be substituted for craft glue.

darning needle – An extra large, extra long sewing needle.

fabric paints – Waterproof, permanent paints and markers that are very good for painting and drawing on many types of fabrics. Available at craft stores.

fake fur – Man-made fur that is available in realistic animal colors and wild brights. It comes in many different qualities and is great for doll's hair.

felt – A brightly colored, non-washable craft fabric. Felt is made of compressed fibers rather than woven fibers. Usually sold in 12 in. (30 cm) squares.

glue gun – An electric appliance that makes gluing crafts fast and easy. However, a glue gun is very hot and should not be used without adult supervision as it can cause serious burns.

googly eyes – Made with a clear plastic top and a flat black disk inside. Either sew or glue in place. Not safe for very small children. Available at craft and sewing supply stores.

grommet – A metal or plastic disk with a hole in the center. Grommets come with craft eyes. They fit onto the post on the back of the eye, after the post has been pushed through the fabric. See "craft eyes".

iron – Some projects require an iron. If you aren't used to using one, ask an adult to help so that you and your project don't get burned.

knits – Stretch fabric available in many weights, such as T-shirt knits, spandex, polar fleece and sweatshirt knits.

loop turner – A very slender wire tool with a hook and clasp on one end. Usually used for turning long narrow tubes right-side-out.

pins – When cutting, pin inside the cutting line. When sewing, pin across the sewing line. When sewing nappy or fluffy fabric, use bead-head pins. They are easier to find and remove.

pliers – Pliers open and close like scissors, but they don't cut. Instead they are for gripping. Use them for pulling, pushing and bending objects.

potpourri – A mixture of dried and dyed flowers, twigs, wood chips and seed pods that are perfumed with scented oils. Widely available.

presser-foot – The metal part of the sewing machine that holds the fabric. It can be raised and lowered and it has an opening for the needle to move through.

primer – When painting a full doll's face, coat the cotton first with an acrylic primer (also known as gesso). It is a thick white paint. Allow the primer to dry before painting the face over it.

raffia – Long, thin lengths of natural straw-like grass. Available at florist shops and craft stores.

satin ribbon – When a project calls for satin ribbon, any type of woven ribbon is suitable. Avoid florist or gift ribbon which is not colorfast or washable.

scissors – Always use good quality, sharp scissors that are the right size for the job. Dull scissors cause more injuries than sharp ones. Avoid dropping your scissors.

synthetic hair – Realistic looking, man-made doll hair sold in craft stores that comes in several shades. Directions for attaching are usually on the package.

T-shirt paint – A fast drying, waterproof paint that usually comes in a sealed plastic bottle. To make a design, squeeze the paint from a small spout in the bottle.

twisted paper ribbon – Its name describes it – wide paper that is crunched. Usually used for large bows. Available in gift wrap departments, florist shops and craft stores.

wooden spoon – When turning and stuffing a sewn article, the handle of a wooden spoon is great for getting into hard-to-get-at tight spots and long narrow pieces.

ABOUT THE AUTHOR

Sheila McGraw re-designed her first doll at the age of three, when she and her sister sneaked down to the basement to give their plaster dolls a haircut and a bath. The result was two upset little girls, one unhappy mom and two bald, lumpy baby dolls. Since that time, Sheila has refined her skills to become a craftsperson, artist and best-selling author. She lives in downtown Toronto where her house and studio are home to a multitude of dolls, papier-mâché creatures, soft toy beasts and her cat Clawdia (page 32). She is the mother of two sons.

OTHER BOOKS BY SHEILA McGRAW
Gifts Kids Can Make (*Firefly, 1994*)
Soft Toys to Sew (*Firefly, 1992*)
Papier-Mâché for Kids (*Firefly, 1991*). Winner of the Benjamin Franklin Award.
Papier-Mâché Today (*Firefly, 1990*)
This Old New House (*Annick Press, 1989*)

BOOKS ILLUSTRATED BY SHEILA McGRAW
I Promise I'll Find You (*Firefly, 1994*)
Love You Forever (*Firefly, 1986*)

ACKNOWLEDGEMENTS

Thank you to everyone who worked with me on this book: Lionel Koffler for making the book possible, Pamela Anthony for her assistance, Joy von Tiedemann for her brilliant photography, Elizabeth McGraw for her hands in the how-to pictures, my editor Sarah Swartz for her super-fast editing and her input, my mom for being a Great Granny, all the kids who modeled for photos and the parents who brought them and to the talented dog Whitson and his masters Richard and Trevor. Thank you to all of the people who work behind the scenes producing and printing this book and to the people at Firefly Books who look after countless details.